Reason, Experience, and God

REASON, EXPERIENCE, AND GOD:

JOHN E. SMITH IN DIALOGUE

Edited by Vincent M. Colapietro

Fordham University Press
New York
1997

LC 97-8014
ISBN 0-8232-1706-x *(hardcover)*
ISBN 0-8232-1707-8 *(paperback)*
ISSN 1073-2764
American Philosophy Series, No. 7
Vincent M. Colapietro, Editor
Vincent G. Potter (1929–1994), Founding Editor

Library of Congress Cataloging-in-Publication Data

Reason, experience, and God : John E. Smith in dialogue / edited by
Vincent M. Colapietro.
    p.   cm. — (American philosophy series, ISSN 1073-2764 ; no. 7)
Essays presented at a conference in honor of John E. Smith,
Fordham University, Dec. 13, 1993.
Includes bibliographical references.
ISBN 0-8232-1706-X (hardcover : alk. paper). — ISBN 0-8232-1707-8
(pbk. : alk. paper)
    1. Smith, John Edwin—Congresses.   I. Colapietro, Vincent
Michael, 1950–   . II. Series.
B945.S7144R43   1997
191—dc21   97-8014
                                                                      CIP

Printed in the United States of America

This book is dedicated to the memory of
Vincent G. Potter (1929–1994).
He followed the Light that guides the quest for Truth:
"In lumine tuo videbimus lumen."

CONTENTS

ACKNOWLEDGMENTS

I would like to express my thanks to Vincent Colapietro for stimulating and enlightening conversations and correspondence about the issues raised at the Symposium and discussed in the book; Dr. Mary Beatrice Schulte for her interest in the project and timely suggestions; Donald M. Levy for assistance in compiling the Bibliography; Patricia Slatter and Linda Ceneri for preparing the manuscript; and my wife, Marilyn, who is Professor of Philosophy at the University of Hartford, for helping to keep my sentences finite.

J.E.S.

INTRODUCTION

Some of us had the privilege of studying with John Smith during what we now think of as the golden days at Yale. There was a rich variety of philosophical perspectives and styles among the faculty; just as important, there was an ethos among the graduate students that encouraged each of us, no matter what our special interest, to take everything available to us with full seriousness. It is not entirely clear that a philosophical community existed among the faculty, who may not have talked to each other all that much. But there was such a community among the graduate students, who found themselves surrounded by both the opportunity and the necessity to become philosophically multilingual. Those of us headed in the direction of continental philosophy worked with full intensity not only on Aristotle and Peirce, but also on logic and the philosophy of science. What is more, we did so not simply out of terror before comprehensive exams, but also out of the conviction, which met us when we walked in the door and which we absorbed by osmosis, that philosophy is inclusive and multidimensional/-pluralistic, as it would eventually be put. No problematic, no tradition, and no method had any monopoly on the philosophic enterprise. Each had something important to offer. For me this experience is best symbolized by my encounter with the *Critique of Pure Reason*. I claim to be the only person in the history of the universe who did not write a dissertation on Kant but read the entire first *Critique* as a graduate student. It happened this way. One semester Wilfrid Sellars gave a Kant course in which we read the Transcendental Aesthetic and the Transcendental Analytic. The next semester, John Smith, knowing that if you start at the beginning you never get to the end, began with the Transcendental Dialectic, and did get to the end. Even at the time it was clear to me not just that it takes two semesters to read a book like this, but also that it was a rare privilege to be able to get two such different and powerful perspectives on it back to back. John Smith was not just one of the resources available to us. Along with people like Paul Weiss and Dick Bernstein, he played a key role in creating and sustaining the inclusive ethos of which I speak and for which I am so grateful. And he did so not by preaching but by modeling. Drawing regularly on his encyclopedic philosophic knowledge, and bringing it lucidly to bear on whatever the theme or text before us might be, he showed us that the only thing to be excluded was the exclusivist posture of any monopolistic claims within philosophy. It was at the intersection of German idealism, classical American philosophy, and the philosophy of religion that John did his philosophical thinking. In that respect it was no accident that his first book was on Josiah Royce. But it was around themes rather than persons that his thinking primarily gathered itself, and among these themes none were more important than reason and experience. So it is entirely appropriate that Reason and God and Experience and God should play such a prominent role in the essays gathered here. They were presented to John during a conference at Fordham University held in his honor on December 13, 1993. Though it is misleading to say so, there is a sense in which logical positivism provided the context for John's thought. His goal was to articulate a concept of experience richer and more inclusive than the narrowly empiricistic (perhaps the ugliness of such a word is fitting) concept symbolized by the notion of sense data and to articulate a concept of reason richer and more inclusive than the narrowly formal and calculative concept symbolized by the notion of symbolic logic as an ideal language. Since logical positivism was the most dramatic confluence of these ideas of experience and reason, John's work can be seen as an exercise in exorcism, directed at positivism and all its works. But it would be better to say, "and all its cousins." For the Vienna circle and their direct descendants had no monopoly on conceptions of experience and reason too thin to satisfy John. So it was not positivism as such, but a pair of tendencies it exhibited with special clarity and force, that provided the primary context for John's philosophy. This is why, in the debate between Kant and Hegel, he found himself on the latter's side. In the philosophical climate where he was working it did not seem that philosophy was claiming too much for reason, but too little; he wanted to show both that reason was not a form wholly external to the experience as raw content and that a reason permeated by experience could be in touch with religious and not only scientific reality. Thus his work is a chapter in the long story of the struggle between science and religion that has so decisively shaped modernity. It may seem that the time for such philosophical reflection has come and gone. After all, hasn't positivism been thoroughly discredited, and hasn't analytic philosophy, once all but entirely under spell of positivistic conceptions of reason and experience, broken free in a wide variety of ways? Yes . . . but. First of all, it may be that the death of positivism, like that of Mark Twain, has been considerably exaggerated. The tendencies here described as positivistic are to a large degree the product of a quest for certainty that does not give up easily. Like dandelions and crabgrass, it has a remarkable capacity for survival; unlike them, its reincarnations are not always immediately recognizable. Eternal vigilance is the price of freedom here as elsewhere. The task of understanding reason and experience, which is to say ourselves, in a manner that approaches adequacy to the things themselves, once again ourselves, is an always unfinished task. Those engaged in that task today can always learn from those whose vigilance helped to create the ground on which they stand, especially when the passion and power combined in the work of John Smith have shaped that vigilance. The second point is simply this—even where there is no danger of lapsing into "positivistic" tendencies, indeed, even where the quest for certainty is so thoroughly discredited that the danger, if anything, seems to come from the opposite direction, the task of formulating understandings of ourselves as reason and experience is recognizably in progress and unfinished. One might say that across the spectrum of traditions, analytic, continental, process, pragmatist, Thomist, and so forth, the common task is to spell out a conception of reason that avoids the extremes of absolute knowledge and radical skepticism. Although they serve as useful whipping boys in polemical contexts, these postures are all but entirely fictions today. Almost no one claims absolute knowledge, either on the basis of intuitionist immediacy or of dialectical comprehensiveness; and almost no one espouses the radical, anything-goes skepticism that says unless we have absolute knowledge we have nothing. Thus almost everyone today is engaged in the very same task to which John Smith devoted himself, that of finding and articulating that *via media* that we might call philosophical Episcopalianism. Finally, it would be a mistake to think that the business about science and religion is resolved. The science primarily at issue is no longer the physics of Galileo or the biology of Darwin but the economics of triumphalist capitalism. In it the secularism of a calculative reason free of either moral or religious constraints seeks to create a brave new world that has already cost more human lives than the Third Reich. On the other hand we find religious forces that seem more the enactment of the will to power than either kenosis or compassion. Ironically, whereas religion once felt threatened by the sciences of Galileo and Darwin, today's will-to-power pieties are so far from being threatened by the form of economic secularism that seems to have won the Cold War that the two emerge as allies (in American, if not in Islamic contexts). This unholy alliance is an important horizon within which we philosophize today. We might paraphrase Kant as follows. Our age more than ever needs to recover the practice of philosophy as critique. To criticism everything must submit. Religion through its sanctity, and triumphant capitalism through its productivity, may seek to exempt themselves from it. But they then awaken just suspicion, and cannot claim the sincere respect which reason accords only to that which has been able to sustain the test of free and open examination. It might seem silly to ask some philosophical projects whether they have any resources for responding to such a challenge. But I believe it is not silly to look for such resources in the work of John Smith. If the essays collected in this volume, like John's work itself, tend not to thematize this political and cultural horizon in which our philosophizing takes place today, we should not infer that this stimulating philosophical conversation has no relevance for that context. I believe it is a conversation with potential to break the bounds of its thematic self-definition and open out onto issues that are more immediate, if not more basic. In other words, I invite the readers of this volume to see whether John Smith's thought, precisely by its philosophical timeliness, does not also have a broader cultural significance than it overtly confesses. Metaphysics is never politically innocent, nor epistemology religiously innocent. No doubt readers of this volume should be apprised of John Smith's long and distinguished career with the C.I.A. Most readers of his work are unaware of this connection, since it is understandably not something he is inclined to announce about himself. But it opens up another dimension of this philosopher, one whose bearing on his thinking can be left to the reader to work out. Those who have ever had the privilege of eating a meal cooked by John will recognize immediately that the C.I.A. in question here is the Culinary Institute of America. *Bon appétit!*

Fordham University   MEROLD WESTPHAL

John E. Smith and the Recovery of Religious Experience

VINCENT G. POTTER

Fordham University

WHEN I WAS A GRADUATE STUDENT at Yale, one of the first seminars I attended was Professor's Smith on the philosophy of religion. I remember that it went for a whole year. My recollection of it is that a vast number of issues were raised and masterfully resolved. I cannot remember ever being bored. That seminar occasioned my first publication in a professional journal. It was on Karl Barth and the proper relation that argument and experience play in any argument for God's existence meant to convince.[1] I think Professor Smith was pleased with it, but in any case his seminar inspired it.

Anyone familiar with John E. Smith's philosophical works knows that among his central concerns are:

(1) the restoration of recovery of "experience" as a rich and full-blooded category against the weak and bloodless account of it made popular by many Enlightenment thinkers; in classical American philosophy, particularly in the pragmatisms of Peirce, James, and Dewey, one can find a correction of this narrow view of experience and so can recover, or, perhaps better, reconstruct, a rich notion from which and on which to build a reflective understanding of ourselves and our world; and

(2) the application of this recovered and enriched notion of experience to our understanding of religion in general and of religious truth in particular; this supposes a recovery of experience, again as rich and full-bodied, against both the sensist theory and, as Dewey points out, against any spectator theory of knowledge. Smith's treatment of this matter is extensive, covering many more subjects than I can treat here. Hence, I will concentrate on:

(a) his interpretation of the phrase "religious experience";

(b) his treatment of disclosure and the idea of God in the context of religious experience so understood; and

(c) his discussion of arguments for God.

I am in substantial agreement with Professor Smith on these issues, but I will raise one or two questions which I hope he will address in his remarks.

THE RECOVERY OF EXPERIENCE

Professor Smith has pointed out in several places that American pragmatism from the beginning attacked the Enlightenment notion of experience as too restricted.[2] For the British empiricists "experience" was nothing but sensation and for the continental rationalists nothing but the immediate presence of "ideas" in consciousness. Smith has pointed out that pragmatists underscored various contrasts which, according to the British empiricists, were supposed to hold between sense perception and reason or understanding. Sense perception was the sole realm of "experience." Such experience was thought of as immediate perception or the first impressions of sense, and so experience came to be thought of as *within* consciousness and even as a kind of veil between the knowing subject and the world to be known. Hence, the pragmatists pointed out the difference between the alleged immediacy of *sensa* and that of the physical object itself. Since most empiricists believed that only the *sensa* are the immediate objects of experience, and since those *sensa* are within the knowing subject, they were forced into a subjectivism which raised the insoluble problem of the bridge.

Clearly, the aforesaid characterization of experience is not just an appeal to naïve experience as lived. Rather, it carries with it a theory indicating what experience is and how much it is supposed to contain. It is crucial at the outset of any discussion to indicate what theory of experience is being adopted and then by critical comparison to test whether that theory is adequate. Smith points out, "It is possible to understand experience in such a way that the rooting of religion in experience is precluded at the outset."[3] He has in mind, of course, the narrow, empiricist theory.

Before proceeding further, let me say that I do not confine the term "experience" to the cognitive. No doubt, to know is an important—perhaps for some the most important—kind of experience, but there are also affective experiences which are had or undergone rather than known, albeit that upon reflection what was undergone may demand a cognitive approach for the purpose of understanding those experiences. My remarks, therefore, will be confined mostly to cognitive experience or to the cognitive aspect of experience. Smith, I think, would agree in that he says in another place, "Genuine religious *faith* embraces both of these elements—belief and conviction—and the two are held together in faith as the *cognitive* and *conative* sides of the full religious life."[4]

As Smith correctly points out, the pragmatist theory of experience countered this drift into a subjectivist interpretation in several ways. One was to show the close connection between sense perception and reason. For example, C. S. Peirce insists that the basic unit of cognitive experience is the perceptual judgment and such a judgment always involves an inference. And, of course, inference is a power of reason. Another move against subjectivism was to deny that "ideas" (whether *sensa* or abstract generals) are *in* consciousness at all, at least not as oranges are *in* a crate. Again, Peirce, for one, would prefer to think that what we immediately encounter (through "secondness") is the concrete singular, physical object. Moreover, all the pragmatists took human experience to be transactional and interactive. The knower is not just a passive "spectator" who merely "looks at" what is going on, but also an active participant reacting to and, in many cases, transforming the environment. Because cognitive experience is itself relational there is no problem of the bridge. There is no "inside" which must be transcended or from which the knower must escape in order to grasp the object itself. Indeed, one can say that "inside" and "outside" have a foundation in the fact that knowing subject and object known are usually not identical, but this does not prevent them from being related; nor does it prevent that relation itself from being known upon reflection. Note that such a view supposes that the real has a continuous aspect and is not simply a set of discrete and absolute items. Interaction is a form of change, but change implies continuity amid diversity. In a thoroughly atomized world, like that of Hume and the ancient Greek atomists before him, change is impossible, as Zeno was quick to point out.

According to Smith, each of the classical figures in American pragmatism contributed something to the recovery of experience. He sees Peirce's emphasis on experience as the compulsory nature of experience and his insistence on the fact that experience is of real generals and not of the representations as a major step in showing that experience is more than sensation and indeed more than just perception. While James is closer to British empiricism than either Peirce or Dewey, still he goes beyond that position by insisting on a "trans-marginal" consciousness which allows there to be more in experience than is being attended to at any given moment. Furthermore, James argues that one should not confuse concrete experiencing with an abstract representation of some aspect of it, since this would lead to the narrow view of experience. Finally, his radical empiricism points out, against the Humean analysis, that experience includes relations, transitions, tendencies, and connectives as well as isolated sense impressions. Finally, Dewey's radical reconstruction of experience stresses the role of experience as an instrument for resolving problematic situations and in transforming those that are indeterminate and unsatisfactory into determinate and satisfactory ones. He insists that experience embraces all that is encountered by the intelligent agent interacting with the world and hence he completely rejects cognitive experience as a spectator sport.

Hence, the enriched notion of experience endorsed by Smith, he puts like this: "In the most basic sense, experience is the many-sided product of complex encounters between what there is and a being capable of undergoing, enduring, taking note of, responding to, and expressing it."[5] Smith and the classical pragmatists reject the notion that experience, cognitive experience at least, can be adequately understood as "taking a look," whether at sense impressions present in consciousness or whether at forms, essences, or clear and distinct ideas.[6] This model must be replaced along the pragmatist lines that experience involve essentially the active participation of the knowing subject interacting with the environment whose being is, in most cases at least, other than his own. While this is not the occasion to elaborate positively what such a cognitive theory would contain, be it said that it would require that what is delivered in cognitive experience be not merely perception but also understanding and judgment, so that cognitive experience both affords and demands an *interpretation* of what is presented to consciousness.[7]

THE RECOVERY OF RELIGIOUS EXPERIENCE

"Religious Experience"

For some time now, and continuing today among many philosophers, there is the conviction that metaphysical and/or religious propositions are meaningless and hence, of course, can be neither true nor false, and so have no cognitive content. Surely a contributing factor to that conviction is that only realities within human experience are knowable and they are what is delivered in sensation and expressible in perceptual language—in a word, the narrow understanding of experience. Professor Smith again has pointed out that James, particularly in his *Varieties of Religious Experience*, and others have tried to give an empirical account of religion by identifying it with a special kind of feeling: the sense of presence, of peace, joy, the holy, and so on. Sometimes religious experience was identified with mystical phenomena of some immediate awareness felt by the individual.[8] These understandings of religious experience are both unsatisfactory and a threat to religion itself. They are unsatisfactory because these various attempts have not succeeded in identifying the specifically religious element of experience (witness the vast variety of candidates!); they are a threat to religion itself because they support the claim that God is nothing but the name we give to a certain kind of human experience. Smith concludes that "the proper contribution of experience to an understanding of God and the religious life may be obscured by the supposition that this contribution must be found only in the special doctrine of 'religious experience.'"[9]

For Smith, religion "is a relation that holds in living experience between an individual person and the object of worship eliciting from us reverence and love."[10] Hence, religion demands an object of worship other than and beyond the self and any finite object whatever. Moreover, it demands an absolute allegiance distinct from any limited loyalties. And yet, Smith continues, "Without some form of presence in personal experience, God can have no meaning for an individual. . . ." In the same place he warns, "but from this fact it does not follow that God or the religious object is *identical* with any finite experience."[11] He insists that there is no more logical reason for supposing that to claim that God is present in experience is to reduce Him to a psychological reality any more than for believing that our experience of, say, a table makes it a psychological reality. The encounter claimed in this sort of situation requires the notion of divine disclosure or revelation of a sort.

The real trouble in connecting religion and human experience is to get a correct description and understanding not of religious experience but of the religious dimension of experience. This way of considering things avoids the difficulties of supposing religious experience to be a species of a genus, in a word, of a narrow and special case of experience. A dimension is not a determining *differentia* but a perspective or an aspect; in this case it is man as raising the question of the purpose of existence and seeking the final purpose which needs to be answered as a basis for the quality of his present life. Smith remarks: "it is essential to an experiential approach that the question of the purpose of existence as such—the question that identifies man as the religious animal—be understood, at the same time, as the question of God. Unless this connection is grasped, the experiential approach collapses into a psychological or phenomenological study of man and the introduction of God becomes superfluous."[12]

Disclosure of God

The connection between the religious dimension of experience and the idea of God, therefore, requires that there be a disclosure of God which, while not immediate, is direct.[13] Smith appeals to this disclosure by likening it to the encounter in our experience of another self. The self is not encountered as an immediate quality known by immediate insight; nor is it known as a universal character known by concepts alone. "A self has precisely the character of being *directly present* in experience and thus of not needing to be inferred, and yet a self is not immediately known in encounter because it must express itself through various media that must be interpreted before their meaning is delivered."[14] Smith observes that while in principle any object or event in human experience can disclose God's presence, there are crisis events in which the disclosure is most evident since they turn our attention to the meaning and purpose of life—those events which point out our contingency, our dependence, our need for something other for our self-realization.[15] Smith discusses at length the claims to a very special disclosure, revelation, at the basis of Judaism, Christianity, and Islam. He points out that in these religions three types of media are found: holy person, historical events, and the natural order. I would like to add here on my account that when it comes to understanding the conditions of possibility for special disclosure or revelation in holy persons or historical events, disclosure of God in the natural order is first required as a real possibility since without it there would be no way of telling whether what is allegedly disclosed in those persons and events is truly God. Hence, I have argued and would argue that some form of "natural knowledge" of God must be possible if there is to be any "supernatural revelation." It seems to me self-evident that in this matter dogmatism is unsatisfactory and an appeal to privileged mystic access arbitrary.[16]

Arguments for God

This brings me, then, to the third and final point I would like to cover: namely, Smith's treatment of arguments for God's existence and nature. Perhaps the most important point that Smith makes in this regard is that the existence of God cannot be deduced, whether by an argument of the so-called "ontological" kind or by one of the "cosmological" sort. The principal reason is that nothing can be legitimately asserted in the conclusions of such arguments which is not already contained in the premises. On the other hand, Smith acknowledges that such arguments, when used in conjunction with an appeal to experience (indeed, to a direct experience of God), are not without significance and vital importance. "The question of the formal validity of the arguments is by no means the only question to be raised; more important is the discovery of the concrete experience behind them and the sort of intelligibility they lend to experience. . . . the argument about God was never meant to be merely a dialectical exercise."[17] He goes on to discuss the ontological and cosmological arguments, emphasizing their weakness but also indicating their positive contributions to understanding experience in its religious dimension.

With regard to the ontological argument Smith concludes that the answer to the question "Is the ontological argument valid?" cannot be a clear "yes" or "no." He argues rightly that a proper evaluation of the argument is not merely a matter of formal validity. The argument must be situated in its experiential and religious setting since it is from there that Anselm takes the meaning of the term "God," that is, from a Christian tradition of experience and faith.[18] If it be understood as an attempt to move from a purely nominal definition of God to the real and necessary existence of such a being, the argument manifestly fails. If it is understood to be a movement from God's possibility to His actuality, as in Leibnitz, again the argument fails, because the only way of showing that God is positively possible is by showing Him to be actual. Hence, if the argument is needed, it fails, and if it is shown to succeed, it is unnecessary. To accept God as actual and so positively possible is accomplished either through faith, as in the case of Anselm and his brother monks, or in some reflection and/or argumentation which shows the need for such a being—what Smith calls an encounter in experience. "What the classical objection does point out is that the apprehension of necessary existence or the grasping of the conclusion that God must be real *does not provide us with the actual encounter* in experience which is supposed to be required for actual, concrete existence as distinct from the rational apprehension that a God whom we have never *in fact* met must nevertheless be real."[19]

Concerning the cosmological arguments, after rehearsing the classical arguments against them,[20] Smith observes that the contributions of these arguments is to make explicit that finite existence is insufficient because it is neither self-explanatory nor self-supporting. One can further conclude that if the universe is intelligible there must be a self-sufficient and necessary being. The demand for intelligibility (principle of sufficient reason) is for total intelligibility; otherwise there would be an infinite regress of finite existents, and their contingency would remain unexplained. Smith worries that this is to argue in a circle: "Is it not the case that these arguments lead to the conclusion of a first cause, a necessary existent, etc., only by the invocation of a principle which expresses part at least of what is meant by saying that God is real?"[21] Furthermore, Smith raises the question of whether the God reached by the cosmological arguments is that of the religious traditions, Christian, Judaic, Muslim. The supposed ensuring dilemma is that either the God of the tradition is presupposed and so the argument is unnecessary or there is no connection at all and the argument becomes *religiously* unimportant. "There is but one way in which this [identification of the necessary being and God] can be done, namely by *assuming at the outset . . . that God is already known to have a nature of a certain sort and that this nature includes the power of being expressible in the world.*"[22] Smith concludes his discussion by saying, "When the deficiency is removed by making the assumption previously indicated, the cosmological approach, *like the ontological in this respect,* can no longer be said to set out from the world alone, but must be seen as beginning with God."[23]

Finally, I would say a word about what Smith calls the "anthropological" approach to God.[24] The issue is where in reflection on our experience can we find the presence of the Absolutely Exalted? They are three: (1) the awareness of the contingent character of one's existence (the from whence); (2) the awareness of the limit of existence in non-existence or death (the to whence); and (3) the awareness of being a responsible being. Smith goes on to say that when man encounters these three points at which his life is related to something unconditional, he encounters the marks or signs of God. The Absolutely Exalted is present in these experiences, and the task of rational reflection is the recovery of that presence through the discovery that those marks are indeed the genuine marks of God.[25] The issue here is to understand the significance of these lived and personal experiences. It is a question of finding intelligibility by an interpretation or reading of certain signs given in experience, and this interpretation is not the same as a formal demonstration or formal reasoning.

This essay is already too long for the occasion, but I would like to address some questions to Professor Smith for clarification, correction, or expansion, whichever seems appropriate.

1. When you speak of the religious dimension of experience other than of religious experience, do you mean that the model

in which "experience" is treated as a genus and "religious" as a specific difference is misleading since it supposes that religious experience is a special kind of experience among others? Would your "religious dimension of experience" be equivalent to saying that we can and should experience the world religiously so that this perspective gives new meaning to every aspect of human life?

2. When you distinguish between immediate and direct experience of God, denying the former but affirming the latter, do you mean to pair them as follows:

immediate = df no medium between two extremes (e.g., knower and known)

mediate   = df something connecting the extremes (e.g., the complex sense network in human knowing)

direct   = df not involving an inference

indirect   = df what has been inferred

The problem to be resolved is that God's existence is the object neither of sense nor of perception, and yet sense and perception are involved so that something else is required for such experiences to be understood as manifesting God. The traditional solution is to say God is grasped by human reason indirectly, that is, by inference. Can we have it both ways, and if so, how?

3. Perhaps your criticism of the various ontological and cosmological arguments for God is a bit harsh, even though I admit that certain presentations of these arguments call for severe criticism. One point I have in mind is your insistence, or seeming insistence, that the arguments in one way or another beg the question by arguing in a circle. Do they? Or at least can one so understand them? I see and agree that the ontological argument needs something to keep it from being purely definitional. But I also think that some understanding of the term "God" as used in English is required even if one does not think it refers to any reality, and I think the ontological approach proves that semantic framework. The cosmological arguments do show in a dramatic way the contingency and so insufficiency of any finite reality, but I do not think that an appeal to total intelligibility is to introduce a totally new principle or to assume God from the outset, for I

doubt that total intelligibility is what we mean by God even if such intelligibility requires that God exist. It makes little or no sense to me to claim anything but total intelligibility, for to suppose anything else is to suppose what cannot even be coherently stated. I assume that when you insist on an interpretation of human experience to make it intelligible you mean that its intelligibility is thus made explicit and we are now consciously aware of it, and, further, that this making explicit what was all along implicit is to encounter God and indeed at that point directly. Hence, I would argue that, rather than God's being assumed at the beginning, God is explicitly discovered as having been present from the beginning. I also would add that while I agree that God is not deduced, formal arguments are necessarily involved in making our experience intelligible and so in our being able correctly to interpret it. Formal arguments are not sufficient for our directly encountering God, but I suspect they will be found to be necessary when the experience is unpacked and explained.

I personally have found Professor Smith's reflections of the proper understanding of religion and religious faith extraordinarily enlightening and very useful for those I have met struggling with the burden of doubt and unbelief in our time. My thanks for the help!

NOTES

1. "Karl Barth and the Ontological Argument," *The Journal of Religion*, 45 (1965), 309–25.
2. See his "The Reconception of Experience in Peirce, James, and Dewey," *The Monist*, 68 (1965), 538–54; repr. in his *America's Philosophical Vision* (Chicago: The University of Chicago Press, 1992), pp. 17–35. See also his earlier works *Experience and God* (New York: Oxford University Press, 1968; repr. New York: Fordham University Press, 1995), chap. 1. "The Recovery of Experience," pp. 21–34, and *The Analogy of Experience* (New York: Harper & Row, 1973), esp. chap. 2, "A New Approach to Understanding: *Analogia experientiae*," pp. 25–43.
3. *Experience and God*, p. 22.
4. Ibid., p. 107.
5. Ibid., p. 23.
6. I have discussed this in "The Recovery of Religious Experience," presented at the Nineteenth Congress of Philosophy, in Brighton, Eng-

land, in 1988, and published in *Versus: Quaderni di studii semiotici,* 49 (1988), 81–89.

7. Hume's criterion for meaning is to trace a term back to the impression from which it is derived. If there is no such impression, the term is meaningless. See *An Enquiry Concerning Human Understanding,* section II, "Of the Origin of Ideas," at the end.

8. *Experience and God,* pp. 46ff.

9. Ibid., p. 46.

10. Ibid., p. 47.

11. Ibid., p. 48.

12. Ibid., p. 56.

13. Ian Ramsey did extensive work on the question of disclosure to overcome the empiricist challenge to religion. In his many works on this topic he offers no fewer than 160 examples of disclosure. The only study, to my knowledge, which gathers together in a systematic way all of Ramsey's examples is the unpublished dissertation of my student Elizabeth Beirne, "Ian Ramsey: On the Logic of Disclosure," Fordham University, 1983.

14. *Experience and God,* p. 85.

15. Ibid., p. 63.

16. Vincent G. Potter, "Revelation and 'Natural' Knowledge of God." in *Neoplatonism and Islamic Thought.* ed. Parviz Morewedge (Albany: State University of New York Press, 1992), pp. 247–57.

17. Smith, *Experience and God,* p. 121.

18. Ibid., pp. 121ff.

19. Ibid., pp. 128.

20. Ibid., pp. 134–38.

21. Ibid., p. 139.

22. Ibid., p. 143.

23. Ibid., p. 144.

24. Ibid., pp. 149–57.

25. Ibid.

Morality and Obligation

ROBERT J. ROTH, S.J.

Fordham University

DURING HIS PHILOSOPHICAL CAREER, John Smith has ranged over a wide spectrum of philosophers and philosophical traditions. In fact, I know of no other philosopher who has more ably commented on the history of philosophy from the Greeks to the present. But through it all, for a long time and almost alone, Smith countered the exclusive emphasis in American philosophy on logic and language analysis, and the return to empiricism in the Humean tradition.

One criticism that Smith has consistently made regarding the development of American philosophy is its neglect of the "broad spectrum of American culture." In *The Spirit of American Philosophy* he noted that one aspect of that culture has to do with freedom and moral values.[1] In his 1981 Presidential Address at the annual meeting of the American Philosophical Association, Eastern Division, after the manner of John Dewey he called for a return "to a direct approach to philosophical issues as they arise from conflicts and problematic situations encountered in the moral, social, political and scientific contexts of modern culture."[2] In his article "Being and Willing: The Foundations of Ethics," he observed that one of the more important consequences for modern philosophy of the emphasis placed on the analysis of knowing has been the diverting of attention from the contexts wherein we encounter the world," and one of these is the moral.[3] In *Themes in American Philosophy: Purpose, Experience, and Community*, he applauded some recent trends in American philosophy, one of which was "a new concern for a normative standpoint in the whole field of value" and a reassessment of the role of reason in ethics.[4]

But Smith has not merely lamented what is lacking in American philosophy; he has also made positive contributions toward con-

structing a viable moral theory. In "Being and Willing," he agreed
with some modern philosophers in calling a theory of morals "an
ethic of self-realization." By this he meant that ethics emphasizes
"the actualization of a whole person through the development of
individual capacities and talents that at the same time constitute
the unique contribution of that person to the welfare of the communities to which he or she belongs."[5] The good has a twofold
aspect: namely, the fulfillment of the individual and the contribution that one can make to the fulfillment of the members of the
human community. Smith also called the good so described a
purpose. As we know, he developed this aspect in his *Purpose and
Thought: The Meaning of Pragmatism.*[6]

The notion of the person's relation to community became an
important element of Smith's interpretation of Josiah Royce. He
described how, after publishing *Royce's Social Infinite: The Community of Interpretation,*[7] he began to appreciate "the later Royce," the
one subsequent to *The World and the Individual*, in that Royce
dropped the Absolute and focused attention on loyalty, community, and interpretation. Smith also came to see that the notion
of community was present in Royce's thought from the beginning, as Royce himself was to acknowledge.[8] Smith noted that
even in *The World and the Individual*, Royce had proposed a novel
idea of being, expressed by the phrase "To be is to be the fulfillment of a purpose." Smith adds: "The idea that will or purpose
defines individuality is of the utmost importance because it figures
largely in Royce's conception of the individual self as an overarching purpose or plan. The self, in the end, is a task to be performed,
calling into play the active powers of each individual." In addition,
"Royce had the idea of the self as a plan or project, *an essentially
ethical task.*"[9] Two aspects are thus included in Royce's notion of
person: namely, self as a plan to be fulfilled, and person as related
to community. Having said this, Smith points out that in Royce's
theory of the self the Absolute remained a problem for the purposive, creative, developing aspect of the moral self.[10] Later it will
be seen how a similar problem can be raised regarding Smith's
own moral theory.

In any case, Smith unites will, the person, and morality into a
single theme. Though knowledge is important, "the world is not
there just to be known and we are not here just to know it."[11]

We become truly persons when we make choices and engage in activities that lead to the fulfillment of the self and of others. This constitutes the purpose or life plan the individual has freely chosen.

In an early article (1949), "Religion and Morality," reprinted as a chapter in *Reason and God: Encounters of Philosophy with Religion* (1961), Smith added some further aspects regarding his moral theory. The article has a different thrust from "Being and Willing," dealing as it does with the relation of morality and religion. But it included some considerations regarding morality which are important for my present purpose. For one thing, Smith contends that morality is *autonomous* in relation to religion. This means that "no alien considerations, such as craven fear of a tyrannical deity or dread or persecution from an absolutistic church, should be admitted as validly determining the conduct of human persons."[12] Furthermore, the principal concern of morality is to regulate one's life in ways that will lead to the remaking of society: "it neither knows of nor cares for the ultimate destinies of the peoples and societies that recognize its commands."[13] Also, considerations of earthly gain or reward and success in life should not be the principal conditions of truly moral conduct. "The good is to be chosen for its own sake, just as the good life is to be lived for its own sake." Consequently, the good chosen for its own sake and the exclusion of craven fear coming from an absolutistic church are conditions that constitute the autonomy of morality.[14]

There is another element that Smith adds. In choosing a life plan, the moral person, the good person, behaves in ways that are considered to be right or wrong. Such a person fulfills obligations and claims, and accepts responsibilities.[15] Accordingly, "the choice of a life plan by an individual must be subject to certain constraints, both internal and external." The person makes a "commitment or investment that is essentially a form of self-identification. It is a declaration, as it were, of what and who that individual means to be, and in the commitment the person places himself 'under orders,' as it were, in accordance with the plan chosen and with the claims of other members of his community to mutual recognition as persons."[16] Moreover, morality entails setting up priorities in making choices among the manifold goods that may be present. Consequently,

No such judgments are possible without principles in accordance with which goals and courses of action are determined and appraised, and principles, in turn, carry with them the character of generality or law. Law is intelligent design guiding willing and thus connecting the person and the structure of the world in which he or she acts in a rational way. Without law there can be no morality, in the sense that being constrained or rather acknowledging a law for "willing" is essential not only for the pursuit of the good but for the exclusion of what is not permissible, what is evil, destructive, and stands opposed to the realization of the good. Morality cannot exist unless there are some acts and courses of action that are not to be willed, or, expressed in other terms, any system upon which *whatever* is willed can be given some justification within the system is no morality at all.[17]

Now, Smith's description of morality is insightful and constitutes a valuable contribution to moral theory. Rich and provocative is his statement that the good life is a supreme end which should be lived for its own sake, and not for any earthly reward. Too often this aspect of the moral life is lost, and the motive for good and right behavior is made to consist in the harmful effects that will follow upon bad and wrongful acts. Also he makes the point that there are metes and bounds regarding what is good and bad, permissible or destructive, so that not everything that is willed is by that fact morally good. Though there may be several questions regarding Smith's moral theory that could be raised for further discussion, it is on the origin and nature of moral obligation that I would like to focus.

Smith does include law and obligation in his moral theory, but it seems that he shares with many contemporary moral philosophers a caution regarding them. As he notes in several places, there are good reasons which prompt such caution: for example, in religion the emphasis on a tyrannical God or an authoritarian church in making "craven fear" almost the sole motive for moral action; in philosophy, the "categorical imperative" with its emphasis on duty for its own sake. The reaction among some ethicians has been to emphasize the attractiveness of the good and its power to elicit admiration and active response on the part of the person.

Certainly one can applaud the move from fear to desire. Likewise, it certainly is the case that action done *merely* out of fear has little if any moral value. And yet there are other considerations that need to be taken into account. Morality does include an ought or obligation which is distinct from an invitation. There is a difference between saying that one *ought* to do such and so and saying that it would be *nice* to do so. There is even a difference in the use of the term *ought*. Thus the statement that one *ought* to appreciate a given work of art is not ordinarily taken to be the same as the injunction that one *ought* to tell the truth. The former has to do with one's aesthetic taste; the latter, with one's moral character. It may even be the case that both the work of art and truth-telling are equally attractive in the aesthetic sense, but the quality of the responses and of the judgments made about those responses is not the same in each instance.[18]

It might be helpful to apply these considerations to the "ethic of self-realization." Surely it is a high ideal which is capable of evoking admiration. It is also praiseworthy for one to pursue the good for its own sake without considering reward or punishment. But what is there in this ideal which makes it moral and distinguishes it from an aesthetic ideal, something that would be *nice* to pursue? One could respond that there is no difference; one and the same ideal appeals to the individual and calls for an appropriate response. The same can be said for the response itself. Morality has to do with acts that further one's development as a human being in a creative way. One makes free choices and performs free acts that lead to one's self-fulfillment and in that very process becomes a good moral person. Similarly, the development of the person has been likened to art and the individual to an artist, whereby the self is created and shaped as a work of art. In this sense, there seems to be no practical difference between an aesthetic response or art and a moral response or morality.[19]

Still, one could ask why one is *morally* obliged to seek the full development of the self. Smith has said that law is "intelligent design" guiding one to act in a rational way. To do otherwise leads to "what is evil, destructive, and stands opposed to the realization of the good." In other words, one is acting in a manner that frustrates the development of human capacities and capabilities. It would seem, therefore, that the moral collapses into the intelligent. But then what *moral* obligation is there to act intelligently in the manner described? One who does not do so could be called unreasonable, but why would that person be called immoral? There seems to be a need to identify more precisely the characteristic that is peculiar to morality, one, say, that distinguishes it from intelligence or even from aesthetics.

Another consideration is that fact that individuals often face considerable obstacles in pursuing their ideal of self-development. Parents often find that they cannot provide for the needs of their children and so they are inclined to obtain money by deceitful means. Young persons may come to realize that, by lying about the character of others in their place of employment, they will be in a better position for promotion. And so they may be tempted to act accordingly. Others may be persuaded by the challenge given to Socrates by Thrasymachos, Glaucon, and Adeimantos in *Republic* I and II to the effect that the unjust always fare better than the just, and that the unjust are happy and the just unhappy everywhere. Socrates would call all these simply the cynical opinions of the "many."

At any rate, they are met in daily life now as they were in Socrates's day. The question can then be asked: Why *ought* one to pursue the moral good in these cases? Is it realistic to assume that everyone is endowed with such high idealism that makes moral action effortless? In times of stressful and agonizing situations, one needs to be reminded that the moral good ought to be pursued because there is something in addition to the inherent attractiveness of the ideal itself. One has the *duty* to act in certain ways, and this duty prevails when one encounters difficulties. Surely, in the optimum situation, when the ideal exerts a strong attraction and the difficulties are minimal, the moral ought becomes almost non-existent. It is comparatively easy in this case to put oneself "under orders," to commit oneself to what one intends to be, to act according to a plan that has been chosen. Smith himself points out the need of perseverance in continuing the development of the self, a task that must continue over time.[20] A renewal of motivation will help, but it seems to me that something more is necessary, and not merely occasionally but often in the course of one's life. And that aspect of morality is obligation and duty.

In his *Ethics*, John Dewey, too, emphasized the wholehearted response to the attractiveness of the good, and he had a deep disdain for "duty for the sake of duty" which can become a fetish. "Conformity to the letter of the law then takes the place of faithfulness to its spirit." But he conceded that at times a sense of duty was necessary "in calling attention to the good which is wider than the immediate convenience or strong appetite." It reminds us of the claims made upon us. Conditions of contemporary society, Dewey maintained, contributed to this need since they had loosened social ties which bound people together. Barriers had arisen between worker and employer, producer and consumer, among citizens in local communities, and between families and the education of the young. In addition, modern conveniences and amusements with their attendant superficiality had altered the center of gravity that held people together. As a result there had been new forms of lawlessness and a diminished regard for duty. Dewey stated that, in the light of these conditions, there was need for "a generalized sense of right to serve as a support in times of temptation." It is a great protection in giving "a reenforcing impetus carrying us over a hard place in conduct." At the same time, Dewey adds, the sense of duty should not become dominant. It has for its function to make us sensitive to the claims of human relationships, to strengthen the will in times of hardship, and to inspire people to develop new relationships "out of which duties and loyalties will naturally grow."[21]

In any case, there is need for a consideration of duty, a reminder that one is truly morally obligated to follow a certain plan of action, and that such action is not a matter of personal choice. It is true, of course, that for the full flowering of morality the individual *puts himself* "under orders," that is, freely makes a commitment to the good and assumes responsibility for its achievement. But at the same time, as already indicated, one also follows orders that are inherent in the moral situation. If that is the case, then a philosophical discussion of the foundations of ethics should address more pointedly the nature and origin of moral obligation.

This brings us back to Smith's early paper, "Religion and Morality," which has already been mentioned. It was indicated that the main purpose of that paper was to show the relation between religion and morality, though there are themes in it relevant to my present concerns. Smith argues for the autonomy of morality regarding religion, but he also maintains that they are very much related. In even stronger terms, he asserts that morality cannot be divorced from religious foundations since the latter supply two essential elements: first, the full explanation of what a human being's final destiny entails; the second, the unconditional validity of standards according to which conditions in society can be criticized. These two elements will be considered in turn.

Regarding the first element, Smith states:

> *Ultimately, no view of the good life, no serious doctrine of what man ought to do, is ever possible apart from some view of his final destiny; and such a view introduces the religious element. This is the most important consideration showing that morality is necessarily related to religion.*[22]

Certainly for Smith religion means the existence of a God and the loving union of human beings with God as their final destiny. In "Religion and Morality," he writes:

> Love of God, as the foundation for the good life, meant for Old Testament prophetism and for classical Christianity a basic orientation of the person as a whole toward the divine perfection and from such an orientation (the same as the Platonic turning toward [*converto*], the light or good) the good life was believed to follow as a consistent expression of the personality whose life is turned toward and centered in God. Hence love of God as the basis of morality involves us in no subjugation to an external authority necessitating conduct through fear, but it is rather the underlying attitude and motive of the person who seeks to live the good life and whose life as a member of society then becomes a consistent expression of an individual will and personality rooted in God.[23]

In *The Analogy of Experience: An Approach to Understanding Religious Truth*, God is the Creator and Sustainer of all things, the Holy One, Father, Spirit, and life.[24] The meaning of person in religion concerns what one is to be, "the ultimate orientation of the self, the focus of unconditional devotion" to God. The moral sphere considers what one is to do, "the actions one should perform in relation to the beings in the world."[25] It would be difficult to find a more eloquent expression of the relationship that should exist between God and the human personality, or between religion and morality. The emphasis again is on love, not fear, on the freedom of internal response rather than external coercion. It also indicates the final destiny of the human being which Smith maintains is needed for morality.

And yet, the same issue arises here as it did in morality: namely, the case of individuals who face great obstacles in living the good life and for whom the motive of love becomes weak. Smith describes sin as "the separation of man from the ground of his being"; human beings by the exercise of their own freedom cease to be what they were meant to be.[26] The return of the individual to union with God is brought about by a renewal of awareness of what one is meant to be and by the use that is made of freedom. Smith gives more than sufficient attention to these conditions.

Nonetheless, it would seem that, notwithstanding the specter of the extreme position of looking on God with "craven fear" and not with love, and the need to eliminate "subjugation to an external authority necessitating conduct through fear," God is indeed the lawgiver and human beings are not merely invited but required to give themselves to a life rooted in God. It is this aspect of the relation of humans to God that I would like to see more amply treated even in religion, though I would in no sense advocate a return to a relationship that is grounded entirely on obligation and fear. At the moment, I myself am not sure how love and fear should be balanced. For example, I must admit to some ambiguity regarding my own understanding of the first and greatest commandment: "You shall love the Lord, your God, with all your heart, with all your soul, and with all your mind" (Matt. 22:37). How can love be "commanded" when it means the free and wholehearted giving of one person to another? Perhaps the injunction signifies that we are obliged at least to examine the reasons why God is worthy of our love, and once these are recognized love will follow. It seems that the command "Thou shalt not kill" is easier to understand; love surely is a powerful motive to respect the lives of others who likewise share an intimate union with God. But the act of killing would seem also to require strong prohibitions.

For all that, there is a problem of accounting for love and obligation in both morality and religion. And Royce's difficulty of reconciling the Absolute with freedom and creativity seems to return in another form: namely, that of combining the free loving response of the individual to God with the obligation under which the individual's loving response is exercised.

The second area of dependence of morality on religion has to do with unconditional standards. Smith expresses it as follows:

> No criticism of the existing state of affairs in any society is possible without the assumption (whether implicit or explicit) of the unconditional validity of standards by reference to which such criticism is made. All critical assertions about human activity of the nature of evaluations (except rigorously *descriptive* assertions) either contain or imply a proposition like "such and such *ought* to be done," and the term "ought" or some logical equivalent never fails to occur.[27]

A question arises regarding the meaning of "the unconditional validity of standards." Austin Fagothey has written about an "absolutely imperative but noncompulsory [moral] necessity."[28] By this he meant an obligation which leaves the individual free to abide by it or not but which obliges independently of any choice on the part of the individual. In other words, one can choose to disobey the obligation, but cannot choose *not* to be obligated. I am wondering if this is what Smith intends by unconditional validity of standards. It seems that he does. In *The Analogy of Experience,* when speaking of conscience, he states that "on the one hand, it [conscience] requires a universal in which the standard—for example, the commandment 'Thou shalt not kill'—is set forth as defining an action which is everywhere and always forbidden."[29] Of course, this standard must be applied to individual cases: for example, to determine if the execution of the criminal or the killing of an enemy in battle falls under the ban. But the standard remains unchanged. In this example, Smith is quite clear that there are unconditional standards and that these are derived from religion.

It must be said that no contemporary philosopher has written on religion with greater perception than John Smith. He also writes at some length and with no little enthusiasm regarding morality. But therein lies an ambiguity, for he mutes his enthusiasm by proclaiming that morality needs religion, and religion of a particular kind. In even more definite terms he states that "morality implies religion and when it is not founded on religion it is continually threatened with destruction."[30] And if this is the case, it would seem that a viable moral theory, without a belief in God and religion as he presents it, is impossible.

Instinctively I feel that Smith would want to moderate this position. He has, indeed, written a good deal about the distinction between philosophy and religion as well as their relationship. This is a large topic and it can be given only a brief treatment here. An exaggerated view of their distinction would look upon religion (Christianity) as primary over philosophy and not at all dependent on philosophy. At best, philosophy is an apologetic tool for theology. The opposite extreme would make philosophy the final arbiter of all questions of experience and existence. Smith rejects both these extremes, and he works out in detail the relationship that should exist between the two. He also rejects the term "Christian philosopher" in favor of "a Christian *in* philosophy."[31] In other writings, Smith has critiqued natural theology, pointing out its favorable and unfavorable aspects in both past and present.[32]

In the light of Smith's detailed treatment of these questions and his prodigious scholarship, I hesitate to initiate a critique of his position even in a lengthy discussion, let alone within the confines of this essay. I would, however, like to comment on two areas. The first is the meaning he gives to the term *religion*, and the second is the need to consider obligation within the context of human experience.

It should be noted that, when Smith speaks of religion in relation to morality, he intends it in a particular sense. Thus, religion comprises not only a belief in God, but also a commitment to the Judeo-Christian religious tradition. This includes the message of God and the relation of God to human beings as revealed through biblical sources and doctrinal positions. It is from religion as so understood, which I will call religion in the "strong" sense, that Smith derives both the relationship between morality and religion and the notion of obligation as embodied in unconditional standards.

But perhaps there is another route, namely, through ordinary human experience so ably developed by Smith, and particularly the experience of moral obligation. In daily life and in a variety of circumstances, one is aware of the different kinds of oughts which have already been mentioned—intellectual, aesthetic, and moral. For example, one deduces that the solution of a mathematical problem ought to be such-and-such; that one really should be more appreciative of an opera or a particular painting. But then a deeper dimension of obligation may be experienced. A doctor on the eve of performing a serious operation will recognize the duty to maintain sobriety. A professor will feel constrained to prepare a series of lectures that have been contracted.

A further advance can be made in the experience of obligation which leads to its unconditional character. This is more evident in one's own case. Suppose, for example, that a person is wantonly attacked and robbed and that there are no witnesses. The person attacked will make the claim that the aggressor *ought not* to have performed such an act. The aggrieved will not be satisfied with the response that, since there are no witnesses and no possibility of an accusation in a court of law, there can be no claim against the robbery. Still less will that person be appeased by the culprit's assertion that he or she simply did not choose to achieve the ideal of self-fulfillment and chose instead to violate that ideal. The victim will still maintain that the robber should not have acted in such a manner and that the act is immoral. More than that, the claim would be made that this is true in spite of circumstances or conditions, in other words, that the prohibition against wanton and unprovoked seizure of another's property is unconditional.

If this experience is pursued further, one can then ask about the origin of such an experience and conclude that there must be a lawgiver outside and above the human situation who imposes obligations even when some individuals refuse to obey them. This is known as the deontological argument. It has a long history which would require detailed treatment. But, as Joseph Dolan has written:

> The argument as commonly presented runs this way: only from a personal being possessing the original and absolute authority of Supreme Legislator can the moral law derive its universally obliging force and man-made laws their own binding power. For evidently . . . only an all-wise God can legitimately prescribe our conduct, witness our deliberations and decisions, warn through the inner voice of conscience, and, some would note, vindicate the moral order with the adequate rewards and sanctions. "Without God everything is permitted."[33]

It would seem, then, that the dependence of obligation and of unconditional standards on religion could be justified by religion taken in a "weaker" sense than that required by Smith, one that would include a belief in a God Who is supreme lawgiver, without the added doctrinal beliefs of a developed religion. It also operates in reverse order, that is, from the experience of obligation to that of a God as source of obligation, rather than the other way around. In the light of these considerations, I would concur with Smith in his pessimism regarding morality without religion, but I would understand religion in a "weaker" sense. Also, while not necessarily calling philosophy "an apologetic tool" for theology, I would narrow the gap between the two.

These, then, are questions which I would propose to Smith regarding his own insightful development of moral theory. Some of them, I am sure, are due to my own failure to understand what he has to say. But perhaps, even if by accident, I have raised issues regarding which Smith is more than competent to provide some enlightenment.

NOTES

1. 2nd ed. rev. (Albany: State University of New York Press, 1983), p. 205.
2. Ibid.
3. *The Journal of Speculative Philosophy*, 1 (1987), 24.
4. (New York: Harper & Row, 1970), pp. 144–45.
5. P. 29.
6. (New Haven, Conn.: Yale University Press, 1978).
7. (New York: Liberal Arts Press, 1950).
8. *America's Philosophical Vision* (Chicago: The University of Chicago Press, 1992), pp. 122–23.
9. Ibid., pp. 131–32; emphasis added.
10. Ibid., pp. 123, 131.
11. "Being and Willing," 25.
12. (New Haven, Conn.: Yale University Press, 1961), p. 197.
13. Ibid., p. 192.
14. Ibid., p. 197.
15. "Being and Willing," 24–25.
16. Ibid., 27–28.
17. Ibid., 30–31.
18. Under certain circumstances, an aesthetic judgment could also be moral, but this case is not considered here.
19. I believe that Smith would resist the identification of the aesthetic

and the moral. See *Reason and God*, chap. 3, "Nietzsche: The Conquest of the Tragic Through Art," esp. pp. 58–61.

20. "Being and Willing," 35–36.

21. In *John Dewey: The Later Works, 1925–1953* (Carbondale: Southern Illinois Press, 1985), 7:232–34.

22. *Reason and God*, pp. 200–201; emphasis is original.

23. Ibid., p. 199.

24. (New York: Harper & Row, 1973), p. 87.

25. Ibid., p. 64.

26. Ibid., p. 74.

27. *Reason and God*, pp. 199–200.

28. *Right and Reason: Ethics in Theory and Practice*, 6th ed. (Saint Louis: Mosby, 1976), p. 112. I have discussed this question in two articles: "Moral Obligation and God." *The New Scholasticism*, 54 (1980), 265–78, and "Moral Obligation—With or Without God?" ibid., 59 (1985), 471–74.

29. P. 101.

30. *Reason and God*, p. 202.

31. Ibid., pp. 134–56.

32. Ibid., pp. 157–72; "Prospects for Natural Theology," *The Monist*, 75 (1992), 406–20.

33. "Law, Obligation, and God," in *God Knowable and Unknowable*, ed. Robert J. Roth, s.j. (New York: Fordham University Press, 1973), p. 199.

Living Reason: A Critical Exposition of John E. Smith's Re-Envisioning of Human Rationality

VINCENT M. COLAPIETRO

The Pennsylvania State University

JOHN E. SMITH HAS CONTRIBUTED to contemporary philosophy in primarily four distinct capacities; first, as a philosopher of religion and God; second, as an indefatigable defender of philosophical reflection in its classical sense (a sense inclusive of, but not limited to, metaphysics);[1] third, as a participant in the reconstruction of experience and reason so boldly inaugurated by Hegel,[2] then radically transformed by the classical American pragmatists, and significantly augmented by such thinkers as Josiah Royce, William Ernest Hocking, and Alfred North Whitehead; fourth, as an interpreter of philosophical texts and traditions (Kant, Hegel, and Nietzsche no less than Charles Peirce, William James, and John Dewey; German idealism as well as American; the Augustinian tradition no less than the pragmatic).

I will focus here on one strand of Professor Smith's contribution to the reconstruction of experience *and* reason,[3] limiting my attention almost exclusively to his eloquent plea for a fuller recovery of what he calls living reason. Smith suggests that: "As regards the nature of reason, we must distinguish between, first, formal reason or reason as purely formal logic . . . and, second, living reason or reason as the quest of the part of the concrete self for intelligibility."[4] It is an error to suppose that formal reason is either the most basic or the most important form of human rationality. "Reason in the sense of living reason needs to be recovered, for it is the form required for all the concrete rational pursuits in which men [and women] are engaged—art, morality, politics, and religion."[5] Whereas formal reason is best suited to deal with highly abstract topics and is best exemplified in such formalizable procedures as argumentation, analysis, and classification, living reason is needed to address the concrete concerns of human beings and is most manifest in such creative processes as interpretation, deliberation, and evaluation. Since "it is the narrow view of [human] reason that produces obscurantism, primitivism, and explicit irrationalism,"[6] it is necessary to recover a more comprehensive vision of what is truly a vital capacity.

Smith's own efforts for such a recovery have been chiefly in the area of philosophical theology[7] and, to a somewhat less extent, in those of philosophical hermeneutics and systematic reflection on a variety of substantive issues (most notably, being, existence, God, time, selfhood, interpretation, community, experience, and religion).[8] Yet he himself clearly suggests that the scope of living reason encompasses more than what he has stated and stressed in these areas of investigation.[9] This scope pertains to nothing less than the most important *dimensions* of human experience. He notes that:

> In addition to all the *contents* of experience—persons, objects, situations, events, thoughts, relations—it is essential to notice that experience embraces *contexts* as well in the *form* of purposes and standpoints through which reality is received and interpreted. For these purposes and standpoints [he uses] . . . the term dimension, meaning thereby to indicate the major frames of meaning [in and through which reality is encountered and articulated].[10]

While he has focused primarily on the religious and (to be sure) the philosophical *dimensions* of human experience, a truly comprehensive vision of human reason would have to be framed in terms of the moral, the political, the artistic, the aesthetic, and the scientific dimensions as well (a point to which I will return later).

PRELIMINARY CHARACTERIZATION OF LIVING REASON

It is only appropriate to offer a somewhat detailed sketch of the historical context (both the immediate professional context and the broader intellectual milieu) in which Professor Smith has undertaken his reconstruction of our conception of reason. This sketch and even the introductory comments of the following several paragraphs are not discussions preliminary to my main topic, but rather at every point integral parts of my presentation of Smith's notion of living reason.

There are three principal reasons for presenting such a sketch. First, to approach living reason in any other way is a violation of it; for this form of rationality is an open-ended quest for maximal intelligibility and, as such, encompasses both the personal and the historical (without reducing meaning or truth to either the merely personal or the transitory).[11] Calling attention to the *essential* connection between reason and subjectivity does not make reason subjective in any thoroughgoing sense; nor does insisting upon such a connection between one's concrete identity as a subject and one's actual locus in history make the subject a prisoner of a particular epoch, without any possibility of transcendence. The insistence upon reason's being an essentially personal drive toward intelligibility does not entail subjectivism; nor does the insistence upon subjectivity's being an historically conditioned reality entail relativism. Just the opposite is the case: objectivity is made possible by irreducibly personal commitments and involvements (for example, dialogue[12]); the conditioned character of any actual feature of selves or their undertakings is accessible only to subjects aware of their own historicity (the actual details of their defining pasts no less than the fateful fact of their historical embeddedness). What results from ignoring these connections is neither subjectivism nor relativism, but formalism. Thus, to present this reconstruction of reason in total abstraction from these two constituents of its actual articulation is to offer a merely *formal* account of living reason; and it is in explicit opposition to formal as well as analytical reason that Smith most often contrasts his own augmented understanding of human rationality.[13]

Second, Professor Smith is a self-consciously historical thinker.[14] He takes with the utmost seriousness the historically conditioned character of all thought,[15] the thought of individual philosophers, that of philosophical movements, and even the patterns of thinking associated with an identifiable intellectual tradition (patterns often stretching across centuries).[16] It seems only appropriate, then, that we approach his own thought in light of this crucial feature of human consciousness.

The third reason is closely linked to the second. Professor Smith has conceived *his own* philosophical project in terms of what he takes to be the deepest exigencies of our historical moment. In general, he is sensitive to the need for articulating a nuanced conception of the temporal flux, above all, a conception delineating time not only as measurable duration (*chronos*) but also as opportune moment or critical juncture (*kairos*). And he explicitly notes that seizing the right moment, or opportune time, "is a function of historical understanding within the context of historical action itself."[17] In particular, a variety of Professor Smith's intellectual engagements (for example, his efforts to free the notion of experience from its Babylonian captivity by classical "empiricism,"[18] to reorient the work of philosophers from its narrowly technical preoccupations to more broadly human questions, and to render experientially intelligible some of the principal teachings of the Judeo-Christian tradition) are informed and, indeed, propelled by historical understanding, that is, by his *kairotic* sense of what most urgently needs to be undertaken at *this* particular time.

His sharp sense of timing, then, is not limited to interjecting the humorous comment; it extends to the major foci of his philosophical career. He has a sense of what our predecessors have wrought and, in turn, a sense of what we need to unmake and remake. And this historical self-understanding of his own work encompasses his reconstructed notion of living reason; for this notion has been formulated, to a significant degree, in opposition to what he takes to be today the dominant conceptions of human rationality (conceptions he tends to associate with the alleged self-sufficiency of analysis, with the self-imposed moratorium on exploring the sphere of importance, with a one-sided emphasis on our modes of *expression* and a self-stultifying disregard of the disclosures of our *experience* in its full range and depth).[19] It will be helpful, then, to sketch the context in which the need arises for reconstructing our understanding of reason in the manner he proposes; it will be especially helpful to present a thick[20] view of these historical circumstances, one calling attention to the resources as well as the needs for revising our conception of rationality. This accounts in part for the amount of consideration given to Hegel in my discussion; for reading Professor Smith convinces one that Hegel's writings provide invaluable resources for both understanding our situation and reconstructing our understanding of reason.[21]

Professor Smith goes so far as to assert that "The most important development in western thought since the death of Hegel is the many-sided revolt which his philosophy provoked."[22] In his judgment, these revolts are understandable and, in a measure, even justified; however, they have been almost without exception militantly one-sided. This, too, is understandable in a way, for how else can one most effectively counter Hegel's all-encompassing rationalism except by refusing to play the game by his rules? One consequence of this refusal, especially important for our inquiry, is that Hegel's vision of reason as a synoptic and integrative capacity has been either rejected outright or allowed to operate only in narrowly and sharply bounded fields. To restrict synoptic reason so severely is, however, a violation of its defining *dynamis*. One might say that the Owl of Minerva's wings have been clipped!

But the legitimacy and value of the drive constitutive of this form of rationality are strenuously resisted because of the unfulfilled promises and, worse, the dangerous pretensions of what today is often called a totalizing perspective.[23] Especially in a postmodern setting, not reconciliation but rupture, not mediation but difference, not integration but fragmentation are what truly count; and any and every attempt at reconciliation, or mediation, or integration is likely to be met with the deepest suspicion. Professor Smith speaks precisely to this point:

> What in the end has been the aftermath of Hegel from Kierkegaard to Derrida if not the celebration of [just] those features of reality which Hegel discarded because they did not fit—*Existenz,* the frenzy of self-will, terror, nihilism, and the absurd, ambiguity, incongruity and madness. But, then, can the error of Hegel be corrected by building [exclusively] on what he omitted or subordinated to the point of extinction?[24]

Put another other way: can the error be corrected by entirely ignoring or persistently ridiculing what he himself no doubt exaggerated, sometimes to a fantastic degree? Professor Smith believes that "the answer is no"; nevertheless, he also does not see "how this answer could have an impact on those who most need to hear it."[25] Even so, the task of reconstructing, rather than deconstructing, our conception of reason needs not only to be taken up anew but also to be done so by those who *are* open to learning some lessons from Hegel.[26] Not least of all, they should realize that "the man who flees is not yet free: in fleeing he is still conditioned by that from which he flees."[27] Paradoxically, then, the philosophers who are most free of Hegel are not those who flee him but those who learn from him. In particular, only those who reconcile themselves to the task of reconciliation are in a position to appreciate the full depth and irreducible forms of difference.[28] Only those who are committed to philosophical articulation in its classical sweep can appreciate the significance of the fragmentations and ruptures so marked a part of human history and contemporary culture.

Of all the exigencies that have prompted Professor Smith to call for the recovery of reason, there is perhaps none more imperative than this: the more narrowly we construe the scope of reason, the more thoroughly we abandon ourselves to "the powers of convention, caprice, and custom."[29] But the dominant conceptions of human rationality, especially in contemporary philosophy, have been impoverished ones.[30] Consequently, it has become more and more plausible for us to assume that an adequate account of human existence is best provided by an accurate description of the clash of conflicting conventions and the collision of capricious wills: we are driven to interpreting our existence as being, at bottom, a contest in which *energeia,* not *logos,* is at stake (as though the two are always and necessarily opposed to each other).[31] Professor Smith's reconstruction of reason has been framed *in terms of* the felt exigencies of our actual circumstances—above all, the exigency generated by our own unwitting complicity in the irrational uses and usurpations of power, though also *in reference to* the intellectual fashions dominating the academic scene at this particular time. Since the fashionable conceptions of human rationality have tended to be impoverished and impoverishing ones, they are sources of the problem, not resources for its resolution. For such resources, we must look elsewhere, principally to the classical conception of *Logos* (including Hegel's Herculean effort to recover this vision[32]) and the insights of the American pragmatists.[33]

PROFESSIONAL FIXATIONS: THE REVOLT AGAINST HEGEL AND THE CRITIQUE OF KNOWLEDGE

Let us now turn our attention to the context in which Professor Smith's project has taken shape. With the constraints of this presentation, only the most salient significant features of this historical situation can be considered. These features intimately concern Hegel; and they equally concern rationality. Given the complexity of the issues involved here, however, I will discuss both these features in two separate stages, dealing with them first in reference to Hegel and then in reference to the topic of rationality.

My suggestion is that Professor Smith's career needs to be seen as an attempt, in part, to win sympathy for the largely discredited approach of Hegel and, in part, to counter the effects of a thriving epistemology business. It is certainly much more than this;[34] but, by calling attention to these concerns, we also bring into focus some of the salient features of the intellectual climate of, at least, the last fifty years,[35] above all, these two: a deep and pervasive hostility on the part of most Anglo-American philosophers toward Hegel;[36] and a deeply entrenched tendency on the part of these same philosophers to deflect the discussion from substantive issues to epistemological questions, usually posed at a very abstract level.

In conscious opposition to this dominant *ethos*, Professor Smith has been animated both by Hegel's insights into the importance of history for not only comprehending but also actually carrying on the task of philosophy,[37] and by an antipathy toward making the critical question in any specific domain of philosophical inquiry (making in the area of religion, for example, the question of the possibility of knowing God) the first and chief concern. He does not think that the critical question is *the critical* question, though he has insisted, on numerous occasions and in various contexts, upon "the need for a controlled or critical procedure in every reflective enterprise."[38] Nor does he suppose that, concerning the enterprise of philosophy, the past is *passé,* though he clearly appreciates the difference between a philosophically insignificant exegesis of an historical figure and a philosophically animated interpretation of some thinker, tradition, or position.[39] (The latter is, in fact, a significant illustration of living reason, for in a philosophically animated interpretation, the interpreter joins the philosopher being expounded: when it is executed authentically, such an interpretation approximates being a collaboration in which the animating purposes are more or less shared or, at least, the futility or misguidedness of the original purposes is exposed by the interpreter.) Moreover, Professor Smith appreciates that the past is of the moment, if only we would insert ourselves imaginatively in the ongoing dialectic of human history.[40]

As we have seen, these philosophical convictions were, to a significant degree, personal reactions against two of the most prominent traits of the professional environment into which he had been thrust. For this environment was, without question, one extremely hostile to Hegel and the style, ambitions, and concerns associated with his name; in contrast, it was hospitable to those interested in devoting themselves, in the most abstract way, to technical questions arising out of an ever shrinking field of legitimate inquiry—especially if these individuals had mastered the most recent developments in symbolic logic or linguistic analysis. Professor Smith's misgivings about this style of philosophizing were as deep as his commitment to recovering "the classical ontological principle,"[41] the principle affirming the unity of the Logos inherent in the world standing over against the human mind and the logos immanent in the very operations of this mind. These are, to be sure, of a piece: his commitment to recovering this principle generated his misgivings about this style of philosophizing; in turn, his continued exposure to this jejune form of philosophical discourse confirmed him in his conviction regarding the need for such a recovery.

In a hostile environment, then, Professor Smith maintained and perhaps even deepened his philosophical sympathy for something like the Hegelian project, at least taken in its broad outlines. Let us explore now two roots of this sympathy: Hegel's insistence upon historicity and his ingenious critique of the critical enterprise itself.

For Professor Smith, Hegel's significance is not that he appreciated, in some rather general way, the importance of history, but that he narrated in detail the story of how, in the actual course of modern philosophy, there emerged a growing skepticism regarding this ontological principle. Moreover, Hegel's importance stems from the fact that his grasp of this development as an integral moment in a dialectical process points to one possible way of recovering the classical ontological principle.[42] (Whether Hegel means more than this to Professor Smith—in particular, whether he shows the only possible or most viable way of recovering this principle—I do not know.)

Though Professor Smith knows he is philosophizing in the wake of Hegel, he does not suppose that he is at Hegel's wake! He is convinced of the abiding relevance of the Hegelian outlook.[43] Though often critical of Hegel's overweening rationalism,[44] he is deeply sympathetic to Hegel's aim of bringing human reason back again to a consciousness of its own legitimate status and comprehensive scope.[45] Moreover, he is equally appreciative of Hegel's insights into the fateful developments of human consciousness, especially in its post-medieval phases. He goes so far as to say that, above all other modern philosophers, Hegel "understood the inner dialectic of modern philosophy [itself] and especially its involvement in the problem of relating thought to the real world."[46] What in particular needs to be stressed here is that, in Professor Smith's view, not only did Hegel grasp better than anyone else the inescapable difficulties of relating our historically conditioned and evolving forms of consciousness and understanding to the actual world in which we are destined to pursue our purposes and realize our ideals; but he also provided extremely valuable suggestions for the ways in which to confront these difficulties. At the heart of virtually all these suggestions is a sense that history is as much the solution to as the source of these problems.

But, until rather recently, the spirit of Kant, not Hegel, has more pervasively and deeply informed the course of philosophy in this century. In Professor Smith's own words, "The Kantian type of criticism focuses on the entrance requirements to the arena of knowledge, the Hegelian type on the critical examination of actual interpretations that have already been entered."[47] Though he himself has maintained from the start of his career the need to move beyond the essentially Kantian preoccupation with the "critical question" (the question of the very possibility of knowledge in some domain of our experience—for example, the scientific, aesthetic, moral, political, or religious), his own Hegelian inclination to take up the constructive task has not been shared by the majority of his contemporaries, especially in the early decades of his career. In reference to one of his own central philosophical (and, indeed, personal) concerns, the task here is not so much to show at a highly abstract level how knowledge of God is possible as to explore in an explicitly experiential way the actual data of living religious traditions. The believer does not need to pass an entrance examination into the arena of authentic knowledge. The presumption of philosophers to be in the position to give and grade such examinations almost always goes unchallenged in the case of religion but is frequently contested in the case of science. In a recent article, Professor Smith observes that:

> It would not generally be supposed that it is the task of philosophy to issue a certificate of validity for the knowledge attainable through scientific procedure even if the analysis of that procedure by philosophers makes its own contribution to the understanding of what science is and means. Why should things be different in the case of religion? The obvious answer is that scientific knowledge has its own credentials and religion, presumably, does not. This view, however, overlooks the fact that religion, while it embraces ideas about the nature of God, man and nature, does not purport to be knowledge of the laboratory sort. What religious belief needs is not to be proved, but to be made intelligible or understood as coherent in accordance with a form of rationality and the deliverances of experience. Proof, if possible in any domain, requires the utmost clarity in the concepts involved in the logical rules. No large-scale thesis about what there is can be proved since the requisite clarity is lacking.[48]

In Professor Smith's judgment, the *critical* turn in philosophical discourse, of which the linguistic turn is in many important respects simply a more technically brilliant continuation,[49] has been insufficiently critical of its own status and, indeed, possibility.

In particular, he insists that: "Every critical or 'meta' standpoint has to face the question of its own status vis-à-vis the objects, languages, or types of thought which constitute its subject matter or domain of inquiry."[50] For much of this century, this question has not been faced as squarely as it needed to be. There was and still is[51] "a tendency to suppose that the critical standpoint represents a 'privileged position' such that when we make assertions purporting to refer to events, to experience, to reality, or even [especially?] to Being we are supposed to be on perilous ground"; in contrast, when we make assertions about the relation between a concept and an object or between an object language and some other language, we are supposed to be in one of two positions: *either* we are carrying out merely neutral analyses, *or* we are operating at such a level that we are not exposed to the same degree or kinds of corrigibility as when we make statements about events, experience, etc. But this is almost wholly illusory; if the expression had not been appropriated for another purpose, this might be called the transcendental illusion! As important as it is to grasp the critical turn as a culminating phase in a philosophical development inaugurated by Descartes,[52] it is equally important to work toward the recovery of a more robust and (in an important respect) *more* critical conception of philosophical reflection.

Hence, against the Kantian approach to philosophical critique (wherein philosophical reflection is, first and foremost, a *propaedeutic* to actual inquiry), Professor Smith advocates a more or less Hegelian approach, one stressing the immanent character of philosophical critique. One reason for this advocacy is that the immanent dialectic of critical reflection itself leads us to question the logical status of our own critiques[53] and the binding authority of the transcendental tribunal from which such critiques issue.[54] While the critical philosopher asserts "the limitation of reason without limit,"[55] the dialectic philosopher (the thinker who resolves to trace the movement of this dialectic and to develop its implications) does not presume that these limits can be fixed once for all; nor does s/he presume that they can be fixed in abstraction from some actual engagement in an ongoing inquiry. That the scope of reason is not only absolutely but also narrowly circumscribed within the realm of appearances (or the domain of sense) is an untenable dogma at the heart of critical philosophy.

Another reason for Smith's advocacy of (broadly speaking) an Hegelian over against a Kantian approach is that the former promises to avoid what the latter virtually ensures—an indefinite post-ponement of a dialectical consideration of substantive issues. The question *whether* reality is amenable to our cognitive capacities was the question that in one form or another "established the epistemology industry from Descartes to Locke to Kant"—and beyond; it led and often still leads to "the postponement of phi-losophy because of the need to know before you know that knowledge is possible."[56] For these and perhaps other reasons,[57] Professor Smith insists that:

> Critical philosophy should return to the dialectical arena. The quest for certainty at the meta level must be given up. The attempt to eliminate disagreement in advance [often by banishing, at the out-set, all positions other than the one being defended] must also be abandoned. Like all philosophical inquiry, critical philosophy must ultimately appeal to *a critical comparison among proposed alterna-tives.* . . . [58]

In other words, the critical impulse might liberate itself from the specific form in which it dominated the course of philosophical reflection, especially from Kant to until very recently: critique must be dialectical, not transcendental.

> Philosophical articulation is inescapably dialectical in the precise sense that it requires a critical arena of discussion within which it is possible to determine how much a proposed categorial scheme can actually interpret in comparison with alternative schemes of the same logical type of articulation. Unfortunately, as happens too frequently, the discussion does not advance to the level where comparison between actual philosophical proposals is possible be-cause all the effort is going into the entrance requirements.[59]

Questions regarding the limits and even the possibility of knowledge cannot be decided from on high, but only as part of an immanent critique in which critical (or second-order) questions themselves are on a par with substantive (or first-order) ones. Professor Smith is quite explicit about this: Since knowing, "de-spite features peculiar to itself, is known as a process among other processes taking place in the world, there is no reason why philo-sophical treatment of that process, including its method, logic, and language should constitute a special sort of inquiry absolutely different in kind from, let us say, philosophical inquiry into the nature of causation, the self, history, art, or morality."[60]

PHILOSOPHICAL REORIENTATIONS: THE HISTORICITY OF REASON AND THE DIMENSIONS OF EXPERIENCE

The main points which we have been examining in reference to Hegel (above all, the insistence upon a self-consciously historical outlook and the critique of any self-enclosed epistemological inquiry) now need to be considered from a different angle, one allowing us to see more directly what is at stake in recognizing the historicity of reason and in delineating the dimensions of experience. For, despite his indebtedness to Hegel, Professor Smith has creatively appropriated these insights; and, indeed, Hegel is not the sole source of these specific insights. The pragmatists in particular are important in this connection, as are Royce, Hocking, and Whitehead. But, regardless of their sources, these insights need to be appreciated in their own right.

First, as I have already made clear, Professor Smith himself acknowledges, in a variety of contexts, the historicity of reason;[61] second, he contests the primacy commonly granted to epistemology. While acknowledging the historicity of reason, he does not accept "some total historical relativity that renders reason all but impotent";[62] and, while contesting the obsessive preoccupation with epistemological questions so characteristic of modern thought and, more recently, of much analytic philosophy, he insists that "an intelligible account of the relation between thought and reality remains an inescapable desideratum."[63] Knowledge itself is, without question, among the data to be explained by the philosopher.[64]

Whereas the Kantian critiques of human reason in its various employments are (more or less) unconsciously ahistoric, the Hegelian attempt to recover human rationality in its classical form is self-consciously historicist. I hinted at this contrast above. But, one of the lessons we can learn from Hegel is to appreciate not only that human reason has a tangled history, but also that this history is effectively the critique of the fateful limitations inherent in the specific forms assumed by human reason in its actual career.[65] (These specific forms are not merely actual instantiations of a more or less one-sided vision of reason; they are also "perennial possibilities."[66]) On one level, this critique is articulated in the medium of philosophical and other texts; on another, it is immanent in the very life of our institutions and practices. For our purposes, what needs to be stressed here is that Professor Smith's sensitivity to the historicity of reason does not prompt him to espouse historical relativism; rather, it disposes him to confront his historical moment in light of historical consciousness, in particular, to discern the inevitable but largely hidden limitations in the dominant forms of contemporary reason, as these forms manifest themselves both in thought and in life itself. He says as much when he states that:

> we should see the impossibility of turning the clock back in order to adopt an ancient position uncritically. *We shall have to begin by taking seriously where we actually are plus the development of the past two hundred years*, understanding the full implications of the rediscovery of the autonomy of reason in modern thought.[67]

This defines a crucial part of the philosophical task today.

As an aid in tying some of these strands together, we might recall Karl Marx's observations that "Reason has always existed, only not always in reasonable form."[68] We might amend this observation to read: Reason is ubiquitously operative, but *never* in a completely or perfectly reasonable form. The universality of reason resides in its capacity to transcend any particular particularity; it is not absolutely bound to assume any specific form and it can attain, in some manner and measure, a critical distance from any actual form it has assumed in human history. But the historicity of reason means, in part, that at any actual moment it must assume some particular—and, thus, some more or less one-sided–form; it also means that once it has assumed certain forms, other forms are, to some degree, fated to follow. To take a rather dramatic example: the Reign of Terror quite naturally, if not inevitably, follows upon the enthronement of understanding as the supreme power over human affairs.[69]

At any moment in history, we are in possession of an historically evolved and conditioned sense of intelligibility. This sense concerns, on one side, our capacity to grasp reality, and, on the other, the accessibility of reality to our minds. Following Kant, intelligibility might be conceived in the minimal sense of that which is conceivable but, in principle, unknowable; or one might follow Hegel and Peirce, maintaining that, properly speaking, the intelligible and the knowable are coextensive. But no matter how we construe the notion of intelligibility, it is inescapable that in our time what counts as knowledge and what counts as reality are issues largely decided for us and (for that matter) behind our backs. The task of philosophy is to help us turn around (an ancient trope, to be sure) in order that we might catch a glimpse of how just this range of being (for example, that range which can manifest itself to us through our senses) has come to count as reality and how just this array of powers (for example, the understanding allied with the senses) has come to count, *tout ensemble,* as the only reliable source of human knowledge. The task of philosophy is, in other words, concerned with exhibiting those "patterns of intelligibility"[70] which, even though they have emerged in the course of history, so dominate the minds of their inheritors that they have little or no sense of the historicity of these patterns. Consequently, the selective and differential claims implicit in any pattern of intelligibility—claims about nothing less than the real and the knowable—can be detected only in contrast to the rival claims of alternative paradigms. Hence, the indispensability of having recourse to a "dialectical arena" in which one categorial scheme is compared to others.

Two points need to be stressed here. First, the various criteria by which the rival schemes are evaluated are not completely fixed in advance of the actual work of comparative evaluation, however secure a criterion (for example, clarity) or set of criteria might be at the outset. The criteria themselves are likely to evolve in the course of the comparison. Second, the purposes being served by the espousal of any pattern are not themselves beyond the scope of criticism;[71] put positively: rationality has a role to play in the cultivation of the ends toward which action is directed. Even though technological control of unlimited scope is often an unquestioned goal of some contemporary societies,[72] the possibility of questioning this goal is omnipresent, notwithstanding the fact that the effectiveness of such questioning might be negligible. (This is one source of the tragic.) In the context of philosophy, the ideal of clarity[73] can operate in such a way as to frustrate, rather than facilitate, the process of inquiry.

The exact sciences are an undeniable manifestation of human reason; even so, they "deal only with those highly abstract features which a formalized reason can express."[74] Despite such limitation, this form of rationality—or pattern of intelligibility—is one of the most dominant in our time. Hence, it is imperative to realize that the restricted conception of intelligibility projected by this specific form of reason entails nothing less than an impoverishment of what we are *willing* to count as reality. The refusal to grant intelligibility in any rich and full sense to the reality accessible to our reason "leads to a most unfortunate consequence, the banishing of the properly spiritual aspects of experience—art, morality, religion, and politics—from the realm of reason."[75]

In Professor Smith's writings, we find expressed a clear-sighted recognition of the one-sided nature of this form of rationality. It prompts him to claim that "nothing is more important than the recovery of reason" in a broad sense. In this sense, reason includes the capacity to frame a synoptic vision, not just the capacity to draw ever fine distinctions; moreover, it embraces the capacity to cultivate a sense of importance[76] and preferences,[77] not just the ability to acknowledge facts; finally, it provides us with the resources for rendering intelligible the Divine Presence, not just rendering explicable natural phenomena. The call for such a recovery flows from a deeply felt sense of reason's being too narrowly conceived and of culture's being too stubbornly uncritical. It is a call addressed to those who have inherited a pattern of intelligibility in which the Logos immanent in them is reduced to the cunning of an animal[78] and the Logos inherent in the others standing over against them is reduced to a concatenation of causes or, less, mere correlations. It is issued not in the hope of jumping outside of history, but in the hope of *seeing through* the historically conditioned and contingent character of the angle from which we view reality and knowledge. But this hope should not be allowed to degenerate into its opposite: though we cannot jump outside of history, we *can* transcend the present sufficiently to free ourselves from the crippling effects of this particular paradigm. The lesson to be learned from Hegel is not "some total historical relativity," but an acute sense of a fateful engagement in which the status and force of reason might be rendered more secure—but with the scope and authority of reason being made more comprehensive (that is, less one-sided).

But the ideal of comprehensiveness (or system) as it actually informs Hegel's project is precisely what makes his defense of reason appear to many of us so unreasonable. We cannot help but agree with Whitehead when he asserts that "A self-satisfied rationalism is in effect a form of anti-rationalism. It means an arbitrary halt at a particular set of abstractions."[79] And we cannot help but see that his assertions bear directly upon Hegel's outrageous supposition to have attained absolute knowledge. Professor Smith makes this point in a gentler way, but makes it nonetheless: "In any attempt to show forth the existence[80] of rationality it is important to avoid Hegel's main mistake which was to set aside as essentially unreal the facts of error and of evil in the interest of an all-encompassing reason. . . . In this respect, paradoxical as it may seem, Hegel did not advance the cause of reason because he claimed too much for it."[81]

After presenting this criticism of Hegel, Professor Smith in one place at least suggests that: "Perhaps the Pragmatists should have the last word here; they saw that in knowing, certainty or scepticism [apodictic certitude or thoroughgoing skepticism] are not the only alternatives and that it is false to claim that if you do not have [absolute] certainty you do not know anything at all."[82] If not the last word, at least they should be allowed a word in edgewise, especially at this rather advanced stage of our discussion! Insights derived primarily from the classical American pragmatism[83] lead Professor Smith to stress (1) the need always to take as the starting point of philosophical reflection some concrete situation[84] and (2) the need to recognize the irreducibly different purposes animating the importantly different, yet equally important, ways in which we comport ourselves. The most important philosophical questions are those arising out of the reflective experience of human beings trying to reorient themselves, after having been disoriented by wonder or doubt or some other disruptive *experience,* toward self, others, nature, and whatever lies beyond.

Our epistemological preoccupation with common sense and scientific knowledge has diverted "attention from the other contexts wherein we encounter the world—moral, aesthetic, religious, [etc.]—which require participation and acquaintance since they cannot be approached in a wholly theoretical way."[85] The recovery of philosophy requires examining all these contexts. To do so, "we must return to the world encountered and recover a sense of the many ways in which we find ourselves involved in it. However important knowledge may be, the world is not there just to be known and we are not here just to know it."[86]

What especially needs to be appreciated is that, in the course of their lives, humans are animated by a variety of purposes; though potentially overlapping, these purposes are often irreducibly different: these irreducibly different purposes are partly constitutive of the different dimensions of human experience; and significant aspects of both the self and the world are disclosed in *each* of these dimensions or contexts.[87] Thus, no one of these contexts provides anything even approximating a sphere in which being is fully and finally disclosed to humanity. One important reason to stress these points is that the differential perspective of the theoretical inquirer, especially one trained in a specific tradition of experimental research, defines but one experiential context (a unique and important context, to be sure, but also a limited and partial one). The failure to appreciate this point has led to gross distortions in our understanding of both poles in experience (self and reality) and also of the experiential process itself (the ongoing, revelatory series of encounters between "I" and "Other"). Given this failure, what otherwise would be negligible commonplaces cry out for emphatic assertion: the self is more than a knower; the world is more than the totality of objects, events, and laws about which certain knowledge, resulting largely (if not entirely) from experimental investigation, can be obtained; and the process of experience is wider and deeper than even the sum total of our informal and deliberate inquiries.

To approach *being* exclusively or even just predominantly in terms of *being known* is to privilege unfairly the differential perspective of the theoretical investigator and, thereby, to denigrate the other irreducible dimensions of human experience. Specifically, to approach being from this angle denigrates these other dimensions precisely as contexts of revelation (arenas in which self and world reveal something significant about themselves).

But living reason is neither solely nor even primarily operative in the distinctive context of theoretical inquiry. Its presence and character are most manifest not in describing or explaining phenomena, not in analyzing concepts or justifying beliefs, but rather in interpreting some series of signs or evaluating the importance of some undertaking. Precisely because the emphasis has fallen so heavily on description, explanation, analysis, and justification, and because justification has itself so often been construed in terms of demonstration, the processes of interpretation and evaluation seem to many people to fall outside the scope of reason. Even when these processes are deemed rational to some degree, it is only insofar as they conform to the patterns set by description, explanation, etc. But the inherent, insistent drive to make sense out of ourselves and our world, the widest and deepest sense we can possibly make, is not eradicated because a caste of intellectuals contests its legitimacy or ignores its operation. And the *various* forms of this insistent drive are also not eliminated simply because only one intellectual activity, or, at most, a small range of such activities, is judged to be amenable to rational criticism; while the failure or refusal to recognize the rationality inherent in these forms can actually diminish their degree of rationality (for example, the tendency to conceive interpretation as subjective in turn tends to remove this process from the arena of criticism), the incipient rationality in all these various forms is never completely extinguished in this way. Of course, it can be powerfully countered and even grossly disfigured. Professor Smith's call for a fuller recovery of living reason than one hears from even such contemporary thinkers as Hilary Putnam and Richard Bernstein is prompted by an acute sense that this form of rationality has, indeed, suffered diminution and disfigurement.

ENLARGING THE SCOPE OF REASON

Crucial for recovering reason's status is enlarging its scope. In particular, the scope of reason must be expanded to include not only the framing of abstractions and the drawing of distinctions made possible by such abstractions, but also the cultivating of "a sense of importance" and (allied with this task) the framing of a conception of the totality. Any truly adequate conception of human reason must be a comprehensive conception;[88] more specifically, it must give due attention to the *axiological* and *synoptic* functions of reason no less than to its abstractive and analytic functions.

Abstractions are fashioned and employed for the sake of articulation (in a sense to be defined). They may, however, be articulated in such a manner that they frustrate, rather than fulfill, the full range of human purposes animating and informing our experiments in articulation. In this respect, there is nothing unique about abstractions: they are like all other human means in their power to destroy, distort, or disfigure the very activities which these means help to make possible. Articulation involves nothing less than making something distinct. This requires using a medium or set of media to allow whatever is being articulated to stand out "as an identifiable unit with its parts arranged in significant patterns";[89] it also demands setting this being "in precise relations to other things."[90] For most purposes, "the multidimensional web in and through which everything manifests itself" is, in its full complexity, safely ignored. Indeed, in order to render things distinct for the vast majority of human purposes, attention to precise, proximate relations might not even be necessary. A vague conception of an imminent danger might, in some circumstances, be more helpful than a precise conception (for example, if I try to ascertain the make and color of the car bearing down upon me as I am crossing Lexington Avenue, the price of precision is almost certainly too high!). But there are purposes for which the most precise determinations and measurements possible are needed.[91] So, too, there are purposes for which it is necessary to go beyond seeing things in their immediate environments and to set them in the most comprehensive context imaginable. One such purpose can be seen at work in the forms of articulation which have historically been associated with both religion and philosophy.[92] These forms have as their goal a comprehensive interpretation of human existence, an interpretation in which the proximate scenes of human striving are not allowed so completely to preoccupy our attention that the ultimate setting of human life receives no systematic articulation.

A hallmark of certain branches of experimental science has been the remarkable degree of precision reached by these sciences. But this level of precision has been made possible by, first, abstracting certain quantifiable features of phenomena and, then, focusing exclusively upon these features. What Royce called "the world of description"—the range of reality disclosed to us from the standpoint of science—is ironically incomplete; it is a world devoid of persons and, thus, of the agents who are responsible for the articulation of reality from this viewpoint. An adequate understanding of science requires going beyond the restrictive standpoint of the scientist; it demands seeing the "world of description" as itself rooted in "the world of appreciation," "the world of purposive and creative individuals who express themselves in novel acts."[93] Scientific inquiry is a purposive activity at the heart of which is an ongoing dialectic of cooperative endeavor and individual initiative, of routine procedure and radical innovation.

If the form of rationality exhibited in the work of scientists lacks the resources to articulate a plausible account of scientific inquiry, then either science is unintelligible or there is some other form of rationality by which its character might be grasped. Of course, Professor Smith rejects the obscurantist horn of this dilemma. Put positively: he espouses the reconstructive task.

So, just as we need a wider and deeper conception of experience, we need a wider and deeper conception of reason. Two important respects in which reason needs to be widened have already been noted: first, the scope of reason must be expanded to include the sense of importance (above all, the critical sense of ultimate importance); second, it must be enlarged to include a synoptic as well as an analytic function. Yet a third way in which our conception of rationality needs to be widened is by guarding against identifying human reason with only one of our distinctively human capacities (for example, formal demonstration) or undertakings (for example, scientific investigation). We need to recognize that diverse and irreducible purposes animate human agents and, accordingly, define human activities.[94] We also need to appreciate the significance of this fact. One crucial reason why *being* has been defined in terms of *being known* is that the partial perspective of the theoretical inquirer has been privileged over all other viewpoints. But, as Professor Smith is fond of noting, being is not identical with being known.[95] The point is not to disparage, much less to dismiss, "the purpose of gaining purely theoretical knowledge";[96] it is, rather, to recognize the partiality of this purpose.

The recognition of this partiality requires the transcendence of this purpose. What Professor Smith says about an abstraction is also true of a purpose: "An abstraction is seen as partial, *not from within* the purpose which controls it . . . but only in relation to some wider purpose which takes more into account."[97] "Partiality is never disclosed for what it is as long as we remain wholly within the specific or limited purpose that produces it."[98] A purpose is not seen as restrictive except in the light of a more inclusive purpose; for example, the purpose of framing a purely theoretical account is revealed to be partial only in light of the purpose of surveying the full array of human activities. Human reason is nothing less than the capacity to pursue a range of irreducible purposes in a self-conscious, self-critical, and self-controlled manner.[99]

It is certainly correct to insist that "The essential contrast is not between thought and action [or theory and practice] but between our theoretical knowledge on the one side and the human purposes which should determine what items are relevant for these purposes and how that knowledge should be used" on the other.[100] It is, however, necessary to sketch more fully than Professor Smith has how our various purposes are to be compared and evaluated vis-à-vis one another. The irreducible plurality of human purposes *seems* to preclude the possibility of attaining what this plurality itself makes a necessity—a unified vision based on a critical sense of ultimate importance. But, at the very least, some greater degree of integration among the various human purposes (that is, the different dimensions of human experience) than Professor Smith has achieved is needed. In general, the sphere of importance is far too important to be left unarticulated. If the scope of reason is to be widened to include the full range of human purposes, and if the task of reason encompasses assessing the relative merits of these diverse purposes in the light of a critical appreciation of ultimate importance, more needs to be said about both the character of ultimate importance and the criteria for critical comparison.

According to Professor Smith, our conception of reason needs to be deepened as well as broadened. On the one side, it is imperative to recognize that reason does not float on the surface of things, but is rooted in the very nature of reality; and, on the other, it is crucial to see that reason in its most authentic sense is one of the innermost drives of the concrete self. We need to recognize not only that reason is the capacity to undertake, from a variety of standpoints, the task of articulation, but also that "articulation is not alien to Being. . . ."[101] There is no warrant for supposing that articulation and distortion necessarily go hand in hand.[102] Indeed, if we frame our conception of being in terms of the actual disclosures of our lived experience, we are led back to "the ancient doctrine that Being is power."[103] More specifically, it is the power "to insist or assert itself and thus to exclude both indeterminate nothingness and the determinate other; to persist or extend itself beyond compression into an instant; and finally to express itself in manifold modes of relationship with others which serve as the basis of intelligibility."[104]

Even though the intelligibility of the world encountered in our experience far outstrips our intelligence—our capacity to articulate it in any full or final way—our intelligence or rationality drives toward an ever more comprehensive and penetrating articulation of what it encounters, unless it is arrested or diverted. This drive defines reason in one sense and also is a constitutive feature of the human self, concretely conceived. Professor Smith explicitly clarifies this sense of rationality and, in the process, connects living reason and the concrete self. To quote a text cited near the beginning of my essay: he insists that:

> As regards the nature of reason, we must distinguish between, first, formal reason . . . and, second, living reason or reason as the quest on the part of the concrete self for intelligibility. In the second sense reason is a living movement of thought related individually to a thinking self; it starts from certain direct experiences and moves toward the discovery of rational pattern and meaning within these experiences.[105]

Living reason does not have its sole or perhaps even its original locus in the individual self. Professor Smith has fashioned this concept to oppose the subjectivization as well as the formalization of reason.[106] Rationality is not confined to the individual self, let alone to a private consciousness. It is more or less embodied in the forms and procedures of our instituted practices (our historical institutions); it is also, in a manner, more or less present in the structures and processes of the cosmos itself.

Even though there are striking similarities, Professor Smith's vision of living reason needs to be distinguished from both what Hegel defends as absolute Reason and what Dewey defends as pragmatic intelligence. Against Hegel, he would deny the possibility of ever attaining a full and final articulation of the whole; against Dewey, he would defend the necessity of framing a conception of the totality in terms of a truly differential principle, one that would enable us to say more than simply that "reality is a quite miscellaneous collection of things related in some fairly constant ways."[107] For any philosopher committed to interpreting the whole in terms of such a principle, questions regarding the ultimate origin and ultimate destiny of the cosmos are legitimate and, indeed, important.[108]

The interpretation of the whole in terms of a truly differential principle such as Spirit provides a unified outlook at the price of plausibility. In contrast, the "interpretation" of the universe along more modest Deweyan lines wins its plausibility by accepting at face value the miscellaneous character of our everyday world; it thereby leaves unsatisfied the apparently imperative need for a unified outlook. But might not the quest for unity here be like the quest for certainty? What in the nature of either our world or ourselves can warrant, at this point, the quest for such unity? In light of the countless failed attempts to articulate a plausible monistic outlook, is not a self-critical form of metaphysical pluralism the most viable position open to us?[109]

In sum, then, Professor Smith's demand for unity seems on the one side too high, and his concern for integration seems on the other too slight. The totality seems to be closer to a miscellany than a system; indeed, the universe appears to be as much a chaos as a cosmos—notwithstanding the efforts of brilliant minds to conceive it otherwise. To demand more unity of the totality than it reveals to us in our experience seems futile. But the reference here to our experience points to the other side of the matter— namely, the necessity to exhibit the unity among the *various* dimensions of human experience. The task of exhibiting this unity, especially in a detailed and plausible way, is unquestionably Herculean. But it would certainly be ironic if such a staunch defender of *Vernunft* allowed *Verstand* to have the last word regarding the dimensions of experience!

PERSONAL PARTICIPATION: A DEFINING FEATURE OF LIVING REASON

Though Reason might not have its sole or principal locus in individual human selves, the most vital form of human rationality is embodied in personal agents and their purposive engagements. It is the self as a unique, enduring center of striving that takes part in, say, moral deliberation, political debate, religious musement, artistic creation, and philosophical reflection; and its participation in these processes obviously makes a difference to this self and perhaps even to these processes. In any event, what needs to be brought into focus here is that "living reason is the rational activity of a concrete self and it means the full participation of that self in the moment of thought."[110] It is the historically evolved and evolving capacity by which the concrete self, in its status as a unique agent, traces the patterns of intelligibility disclosed in its experience and attempts to integrate the patterns emerging from the various contexts of human experience.

In this process, the self recognizes its own status as a rational agent. Moreover, s/he feels, at once, the force of unconditional demands and the presence of an apparently unlimited freedom, at least insofar as the self can exercise its freedom in such a way as to ignore the demands which s/he actually feels. For such a self, "There is no sense of external compulsion and no sense of being determined by a merely formal necessity."[111] There might be an imperative *personal* need ("Here I stand; I cannot do otherwise"), but this need is felt to be in accord with the self's innermost nature. That, given these premises, the conclusion cannot be otherwise is a pattern or relationship accessible to purely formal reason; that I cannot do otherwise than accept this conclusion is a more complicated affair, one involving my identification with specific procedures as well as general norms (not to mention overarching ideals such as truth). This more complicated affair is comprehensible only to living reason.

But this way of marking the difference does not adequately get at this difference, for it is the ineliminably personal relationship of the self to the subject matter being explored and articulated that is of the utmost significance. Formal reason is operative in those cases in which the relationship of the self to the subject matter at hand can be safely ignored (indeed, there might be definite advantages to leaving the personal dimension out of the picture). Living reason is employed in those instances in which this relationship of the essence—in which *this* concrete self and *this* subject matter—is mutually implicated. Often this relationship takes the form of a fateful struggle in which the self is acutely conscious of the fact that, in supporting or resisting this way, in accepting or rejecting this job, its very identity is being defined.

Just as in the case of history, so too here what is often taken to be the source of the problem can be viewed as providing the resources for addressing the problem. It is precisely as historically conscious agents that we transcend, in some manner and measure, our historically conditioned patterns of intelligibility and conduct; likewise, it is as self-conscious and (in a sense) self-responsible participants in some rational pursuit that the very rationality of the undertaking is established and sustained. The consciousness of history no more rules out the transcendence of history than the presence of the rational self in its characteristic pursuits eliminates the rationality of these enterprises (by making them subjective, or arbitrary, or capricious). Only by attending to our actual historical conditions can we transcend those conditions; and only by acknowledging our ineliminable personal presence in our rational pursuits can these pursuits more fully embody their inherent rationality and realize their constitutive ideals.

Professor Smith's call for a fuller recovery of living reason is, in some important respects, close to the call issued by Emerson. In particular, it is close to that side of Emerson in which verbal articulation (expression) is subordinated to personal participation (experience consequent upon engagement): "The man thinks he can know this or that, by words and writing. It can only be known or done organically. He must plunge into the universe, and live in its forms—sink to rise. None any work can frame unless himself become the same."[112] In Professor Smith no less than in Emerson, one encounters a drive toward reconciliation, toward overcoming the forms of estrangement so deeply rooted in later modern ways of thinking and, indeed, living. Possibilities for participating in the life of one's culture in such a way as to be enhanced, rather than alienated, is what living reason must, above all, envision.

Unlike Emerson, however, Professor Smith vigorously defends some of the traditional forms of religious worship. The estrangement from these forms is what needs to be overcome. It is in reference to this task that he most fully explores his highly suggestive notion of living reason. One significant outcome of this exploration is that, concerning the reality and nature of God, the emphasis shifts *from* proof (providing evidence for what is allegedly not present or manifest) to intelligibility (rendering comprehensible that which is directly encountered but not immediately cognizable). And one important result of this shift in emphasis is that the interpretive and conciliatory functions of living reason tend to eclipse somewhat the evidential and critical functions. In his concern to counter any and all tendencies to uproot living reason from its meditative context (cf. Anselm), Professor Smith perhaps drives too deep a wedge between intelligibility and proof; moreover, in his insistence upon the irreducibility of the categories of self and purpose, the propriety and indeed indispensability of the impersonal modes of discourse and objective tests for our claims are perhaps also not sufficiently appreciated.

When we turn from the religious to other dimensions of human experience, it should become apparent that a truly comprehensive vision of human reason would need to be framed not simply in terms of intelligibility but also and more broadly in terms of an evolving set of intersecting ideals. The task of envisioning human rationality in this light is one of the most significant contributions that we who are rooted in classical American philosophy can make to contemporary philosophy (cf. Putnam and Bernstein). We are in an advantageous position to execute this task since within this rich tradition *both* the drive to frame a synoptic vision and the demand to respect irreducible plurality coexist; beyond this, this drive and this demand generate a creative tension.

CONCLUSION

From John E. Smith's earliest writings to his most recent, we not only hear a call for a recovery of reason but also can observe significant steps toward this recovery. We learn important lessons about human reason in its most authentic form. The tendency to conceive reason exclusively in terms of analysis, the tendency to take the indispensable business of framing abstractions as the whole business (thereby ignoring the at least equally vital task of recovering, via abstractions and articulation, concreteness), the tendency to link authenticity with immediacy (thereby putting authenticity against articulation and, more specifically, interpretation), the tendency to treat rationality as the power to transcend history or (the mirror-image error) as the power to cope with the merely contingent tangles of a completely insular movement, the tendency to tie reason to the quest for apodictic certitude, and (finally) the tendency to construe the task of reason as framing perspectives or approaches for which rivals or alternatives are ruled out of court—these are all tendencies that Professor Smith has challenged throughout his career. A positive, coherent, and compelling vision of reason emerges out of his critiques of these tendencies—a vision of reason as dialectical, historical, hermeneutical, fallibilistic, contextual, participatory, and conciliatory. For John E. Smith, reason is *dialectical* (ever concerned with the critical comparison of alternative perspectives), *historical* (ever attentive to the way these perspectives take shape as the working viewpoints of actual intellectual traditions), *interpretive* or *hermeneutic* (ever dissatisfied with appeals to immediacy when these foreclose or undermine—rather than open and foster—the possibilities for wider and deeper interpretations), *fallibilistic* (ever mindful of its own liability to error, distortion, and one-sidedness), *contextual* (ever concerned to bring into focus the actual contexts of our interpretive endeavors, thus to bring to fuller and finer awareness the purposes constitutive of these contexts), *participatory* (ever appreciative of the way human agents acquire their distinctive competencies and excellences in and through their participation in traditional practices), and *conciliatory* (ever sensitive to the ways these agents can become uprooted from sustaining traditions, and, moreover, ever concerned to identify possibilities for overcoming or at least countering the forms of alienation inherent in the dialectic of participation and deracination).

Very few tasks, if any at all, are more important than the recovery of reason in the sense indicated here. But central to such a recovery is the fuller explication of the origin, status, nature, and scope of living reason. If my comments and challenges assist Professor Smith and (for that matter) others in explicating these facets of rationality, my most immediate objective will be attained; if these explications prove in time truly to illuminate more fully than hitherto these facets, then an even more significant purpose will be fulfilled.

NOTES

1. One of his most eloquent calls for the recovery of philosophy in this sense is his Presidential Address in 1981 to the Eastern Division of the American Philosophical Association. It can be found in the revised edition of *The Spirit of American Philosophy* (Albany: State University of New York Press, 1983), pp. 223–42.

2. It might seem odd to speak of Hegel as having inaugurated a reconstruction of experience no less than of reason (*Vernunft*). But, as Professor Smith himself points out, "Hegel had a high regard for the empirical principle in philosophy, although he could not accept the classical British empiricism and its narrow view of the nature of experience" ("The Relation of Thought and Being: Some Lessons from Hegel's *Encyclopedia,*" *The New Scholasticism,* 38 [1964], 22–43). Hegel himself is quite explicit on this point (see, for example, *Logic: Part One of the Encyclopaedia of the Philosophical Sciences,* trans. William Wallace [Oxford: Clarendon, 1975], pp. 16–18).

Though highly critical of Hegel's overweening rationalism, William James stresses not so much Hegel's theoretical appreciation of the empirical principle as his empirical acuity. He goes so far as to claim that Hegel was "a naïvely observant man" who "plants himself in the empirical flux of things and gets the impression of what happens" (*A Pluralistic Universe* [Cambridge, Mass.: Harvard University Press, 1977], p. 44). When Hegel did so, his observations are of the utmost value: "Merely as a reporter of certain empirical aspects of the actual, Hegel, then, is great and true" (*Pluralistic Universe,* p. 49). As far as I can discern, Smith shares this assessment of Hegel; and though he himself is critical of the overweening rationalism evident in Hegel's philosophical project, he feels that the failure of refusal to frame a comprehensive vision is lamentable.

3. It deserves to be noted that the reconstruction of experience is closely linked to that of reason and that this twin task is itself closely allied to advancing the cause of philosophy in its classical sense: "If philosophy is to recover itself in our time and acquire a voice that will contribute something to the illumination and resolution of contemporary human questions, it will have . . . to recover a broader conception of experience and reason, so that the former is no longer represented by droplets of sense, and the latter by formalized logic, for on such a basis the richness of experience is lost and such an empty reason is ill-equipped to deal with all [any of?] the important issues of ethics, metaphysics, and religion" (*Spirit of American Philosophy*, pp. 221–22).

4. *Experience and God* (New York: Oxford University Press, 1968; repr. New York: Fordham University Press, 1995), p. 111.

5. Ibid., p. 112. Cf. "Relation of Thought and Being," 31.

6. *America's Philosophical Vision* (Chicago: The University of Chicago Press, 1992), p. 118.

7. "Prospects for Natural Theology," *The Monist*, 75, No. 3 (July 1992), 406.

8. Each of these areas perhaps needs to be explained more fully or, at least, illustrated. By *philosophical hermeneutics*, I mean Smith's philosophical interpretation of such philosophical texts as Hegel's *Logic*, Peirce's "A Neglected Argument for the Reality of God," virtually the whole of Royce's writings, etc. In these interpretative essays, he is doing more than explicating the meaning of texts: often (perhaps usually) he is presenting views that deserve a wider and fairer hearing than they tend to receive. Very often, he is, via his interpretations no less than his critiques, in effect presenting and even in a measure defending views close to his own. Often these bear directly on the nature and scope of rationality (see, for example, *Reason and God* [New Haven, Conn.: Yale University Press, 1961], chap. 5; "Relation of Thought and Being"; *Purpose and Thought: The Meaning of Pragmatism* [New Haven, Conn.: Yale University Press, 1978], esp. chaps. 4 and 5; and *America's Philosophical Vision*, pp. 81–84).

Smith himself sharply distinguishes between natural theology and philosophical theology, meaning by the latter the systematic efforts of an historically informed and, indeed, shaped rationality to render intelligible the content implicit in the teachings, symbols, and practices of particular religious traditions. He contends that: "The historical situation of all thought entails that it will be affected and informed by the cultural substance, including the religion or religions of a people. If this is so, can we still speak about a 'pure' or 'unaided' reason that somehow stands apart from the influence at the hands of the same revealed faith from which it is to be distinguished?" ("Prospects for Natural Theology," 409). It is significant that it is here, in reference to philosophical theology, that we encounter his most detailed discussions of living reason.

Finally, there are a number of essays—for example, "Being, Immediacy, and Articulation" (*Review of Metaphysics*, 24, No. 4 [June 1971], 593–613), "Interpreting Across Boundaries" (in *Understanding the Chinese Mind*, ed. Robert E. Allison [Hong Kong: Oxford University Press, 1989], pp. 26–47), "The Reflexive Turn" and "The Critique of Abstractions and the Scope of Reason" (*America's Philosophical Vision*, chaps. 5 and 6, respectively)—in which substantive issues are addressed in a systematic manner. One of his students, Robert Neville, has criticized Smith for relying almost exclusively on the philosophical essay as a vehicle for his systematic work ("John E. Smith as Jeremiah," *Transactions of the Charles S. Peirce Society*, 22, No. 3 [Summer 1986], 263–65; for Smith's defense of himself, see "Response [to Andrew Reck and Robert Neville]," *Transactions of the Charles S. Peirce Society*, 22, No. 3 [Summer 1986], 273–88). There is, no doubt, something regrettable in this. Even so, some of Smith's essays need to be seen for what they so clearly are: important contributions to systematic philosophy.

9. *Experience and God*, p. 112; *America's Philosophical Vision*, p. 118.

10. "Philosophical Interpretation and the Religious Dimension of Experience," *Logos*, 2 (1981), 9; *Experience and God*, pp. 36ff.

11. This is, in my judgment, clearly implicit in Smith's insistence that not "every form of articulation requires the thinker to cancel his own relation as an individual to what is articulated" ("Being, Immediacy, and Articulation," 606). Indeed, some forms of articulation, including the philosophical and the religious, demand that we thematize our various and tangled relationships as individuals to what we are trying to articulate. This insistence suggests a deep affinity between Professor Smith's own outlook and the personalist tradition, a tradition which should be viewed not as an insignificant footpath off the highway of philosophical idealism but rather, perhaps, as one of the most promising trajectories within the idealistic tradition.

12. Cf. *Spirit of American Philosophy*, pp. 26ff., and "History of Science and the Ideal of Scientific Objectivity," *Revue Internationale de Philosophie*, 99–100 (1972), 172–86.

13. See, for example, *Experience and God*, p. 112.

14. See, for example, "Time, Times, and the 'Right Time': *Chronos* and *Kairos*," *The Monist*, 53 (1969), 1–13; "Time and Qualitative Time,"

Review of Metaphysics, 60, No. 1 (1986), 3–16; *America's Philosophical Vision*, pp. 85–86.

15. "Prospects for Natural Theology," 406–407.

16. *America's Philosophical Vision*, p. 86.

17. "Time, Times, and the 'Right Time,'" 12.

18. "Philosophical Interpretation and the Religious Dimension of Experience," 8.

19. Though Professor Smith always grants primacy to experience over expression, his view of the relationship between the two is nuanced and, indeed, dialectical. What he most strenuously insists upon is that "Experience drives toward expression . . . but there is no corresponding drive in the opposite direction" (*Experience and God*, p. 13). In another place, he develops this point as follows: "*Experience . . .* demands *expression. . . .* Experience and expression can be distinguished as can be seen from the need to avoid confusing a sign with what it means or with the object to which it refers. The two, however, cannot be separated since they are intertwined so closely that we cannot have one without the other. Experience, nevertheless, must not be subordinated to language since it is to experience that we must continually return in order to access the adequacy and accuracy of its expression" ("Interpreting Across Boundaries," pp. 27–28; cf. *Experience and God*, pp. 12–13, and "Being and Willing: The Foundation of Ethics," *Journal of Speculative Philosophy*, 1, No. 1 (1987), 24.

20. Though this adjective has become a fashionable term in contemporary philosophical discourse, it is only fitting to recall here that James himself was fond of this locution. In one place, he noted that: "Among the philosophic cranks of my acquaintance in the past was a lady all the tenets of whose system I have forgotten except one. Had she been born in the Ionian archipelago some three thousand years ago, that one doctrine would probably have made her name sure in every university curriculum and examination paper. The world, she said, is composed of only two elements, the Thick, namely, and the Thin. No one can deny the truth of this analysis, as far as it goes (tho in light of our contemporary knowledge of nature it has itself a rather 'thin' sound), and it is nowhere truer than in that part of the world called philosophy" (*Pluralistic Universe*, p. 64).

21. Cf. Merold Westphal, *Hegel, Freedom, and Modernity* (Albany: State University of New York Press, 1992).

22. "Being, Immediacy, and Articulation," 593.

23. See Richard J. Bernstein, *The New Constellation* (Cambridge, Mass.: The MIT Press, 1992). chap. 2.

Jean-François Lyotard's concluding sentences of *The Postmodern Con-*

dition have virtually become a *locus classicus* of this postmodern sensibility: "We have paid a high enough price for the nostalgia of the whole and the one, for the reconciliation of the concept and the sensible, of the transparent and the communicable experience. Under the general demand for slackening and for appeasement, we can hear the mutterings of the desire for a return of terror, for the realization of the fantasy to seize reality. The answer is: Let us wage a war on totality; let us be witnesses to the unpresentable; let us activate the differences and save the honor of the name [presumably, the particular as such]" (trans. Geoff Bennington and Brian Massumi [Minneapolis: University of Minnesota Press, 1984], pp. 81–82).

24. "Response [to Andrew Reck and Robert Neville]," 286.

25. Ibid.

26. Certainly, that one of Professor Smith's articles bears the title "The Relation between Thought and Being: Some Lessons from Hegel's *Encyclopedia*" turns out, in light of his tendency to return again and again to these lessons (for example, "Response [to Andrew Reck and Robert Neville]", 282–83), to be of fundamental significance. He has been trying to present these lessons to a largely resistant philosophical public, a fact discussed at length later in my essay.

27. Hegel, *Logic*, p. 138.

28. For a vivid illustration of this, see Smith, "Interpreting Across Boundaries."

29. "Relation of Thought and Being," 31; *Spirit of American Philosophy*, pp. 219–22.

In *Reconstruction in Philosophy* (1920), Dewey claims that "The causes remain which brought philosophy into existence as an attempt to find an intelligent substitute for blind custom and blind impulse as guides to life and conduct. The attempt has not been successfully accomplished. Is there not reason for believing that the release of philosophy from its burden of sterile metaphysics and sterile epistemology instead of depriving philosophy of problems and subject-matter would open a way to questions of the most perplexing and the most significant sort?" (in *John Dewey: The Middle Works, 1899–1924* [Carbondale: Southern Illinois University Press, 1982], 12:152.) Professor Smith would agree, I believe, with the initial observation but want to resist to some extent the full force of Dewey's rhetorical question; for him, Dewey's dismissal of "vain metaphysics and idle epistemology" licenses jettisoning too much of our philosophical heritage and draws too sharp a distinction between the problems of men and women, on the one hand, and those of philosophers and theologians, on the other. Much metaphysics has been vain speculation, but less (perhaps far less) than Dewey supposes; and, of even greater significance, some of the questions which Dewey himself in effect suppresses are precisely those that need to be confronted if we are to be in the position to engage effectively in just the tasks which Dewey finds so pressing (*America's Philosophical Vision*, pp. 115–16). Much epistemology has been idle reflection; Smith agrees more with Dewey's untiring attack on the epistemology industry than with Dewey's rather undiscriminating disparagement of traditional metaphysics. Even so, he questions one of the principal ways in which Dewey tries to delimit the proper sphere of epistemological inquiry: namely, by drawing an extremely sharp distinction between *having* and *knowing* (such that experience is, first and foremost, an affair of having in which problematic situations inevitably emerge and call forth inquiry (*Purpose and Thought*, pp. 151–52; cf. *Reason and God*, pp. 107ff.).

30. See, for example, *America's Philosophical Vision*, pp. 40, 88, 118.

31. The immense prestige that Friedrich Nietzsche and Michel Foucault enjoy today is related to this particular emphasis in contemporary thought. Because their outlooks focus on the agonistic dimension of human existence, they are presumed to be (to use one of Professor Smith's own expressions) "down at headquarters." It is only fitting to note here that Professor Smith has written an insightful essay on Nietzsche, one which concludes with a critique bearing upon this precise point (*Reason and God*, pp. 60–61).

32. "Relation of Thought and Being," 25; "Being, Immediacy, and Articulation," 594; "Response [to Andrew Reck and Robert Neville]," 283–88.

33. "Response [to Andrew Reck and Robert Neville]," 286.

34. Two important respects in which it is more than this might be made by plumbing the significance of the two points being stressed here: the defense of Hegel is in effect a defense of human reason as a synoptic power; the critique of the epistemology industry is a plea for a more straightforward engagement in substantive philosophical investigation.

35. See his "A Fifty-Year Retrospective in Philosophy," *International Philosophical Quarterly*, 21, No. 2 (June 1981), 123–32.

36. Richard J. Bernstein, "Why Hegel Now?" *Philosophical Profiles* (Philadelphia: University of Pennsylvania Press, 1986), pp. 141, 147, 150, 156.

37. One consequence of this has been that his contributions have been dismissed by some representatives of mainstream analytic philosophy as "historical" rather than "philosophical," as though the two were separable. In light of this, his call for initiating a more inclusive community of philosophical inquirers needs to be seen for what it is—a gracious and generous gesture (*Spirit of American Philosophy*, pp. 241–42).

38. "Fifty-Year Retrospective in Philosophy," 125.

39. *Reason and God*, p. 107.

40. William Ernest Hocking, *What Man Can Make of Man* (New York: Harper & Bros., 1942), pp. 1–7.

41. "Relation of Thought and Being," 38.

42. "Response [to Andrew Reck and Robert Neville]," 283–86.

43. Cf. Bernstein, "Why Hegel Now?" and *The New Constellation* (Cambridge, Mass.: The MIT Press, 1992).

44. See, for example, "Relation of Thought and Being," 33, 41; "Response [to Andrew Reck and Robert Neville]," 286.

45. "Relation of Thought and Being," 35.

46. Ibid.

47. "Hegel's Critique of Kant," *Review of Metaphysics*, 26, No. 3 (March, 1973), 445; cf. 443.

48. "Prospects for Natural Theology," 412.

49. "Fifty-Year Retrospective in Philosophy," 123.

50. *America's Philosophical Vision*, p. 100.

51. Professor Smith thinks that this situation still obtains. In a recently published article on "Prospects for Natural Theology," he suggests that "Hegel sought to recover the rights of reason, but as Charles Taylor has pointed out, the viability of Hegel's approach is greatly weakened by the fact that *in our present climate of opinion* it is understanding and not reason that holds sway" (408; emphasis added).

52. See, for example, "Relation of Thought and Being," 35–36.

53. "Hegel's Critique of Kant," 444.

54. Ibid., 457–60.

55. Ibid., 459.

56. "Response [to Andrew Reck and Robert Neville]," 283.

57. Cf. "Fifty-Year Retrospective on Philosophy."

58. *America's Philosophical Vision*, p. 101; emphasis added.

59. "Being, Immediacy, and Articulation," 609–10.

60. *America's Philosophical Vision*, p. 100.

61. See, for example, "Prospects for Natural Theology," 406–407.

62. Ibid., 407.

63. "Relation of Thought and Being," 26.

64. Ibid.

65. Alasdair MacIntyre, *A Short History of Ethics* (New York: Macmillan, 1966), p. 203.

66. See, for example, "Relation of Thought and Being," 27.

67. Ibid., 43; emphasis added.

68. *The Marx–Engels Reader*, ed. Robert C. Tucker, 2nd ed. (New York: Norton, 1978), p. 14.

69. Westphal, *Hegel, Freedom, and Modernity*, chap. 6.

70. Smith, "The Two Journeys to the Divine Presence," in *The Universe as Journey: Conversations with W. Norris Clarke, S.J.*, ed. Gerald McCool, s.j. (New York: Fordham University Press, 1988), p. 143.

71. Cf. *America's Philosophical Vision*, pp. 39, 46.

72. Cf. ibid., p.45.

73. "The Philosophy and Religion," in *The Great Ideas Today*, ed. R. M. Hutchins and M. J. Adler (Chicago: Encyclopedia Britannica, 1965), p. 217.

74. "Relation of Thought and Being," 31.

75. Ibid.; cf. *America's Philosophical Vision*, p. 118.

76. *America's Philosophical Vision*, p. 118.

77. "Being and Willing," 32.

78. Cf. Alfred North Whitehead, *The Function of Reason* (Princeton, N.J.: Princeton University Press, 1929), p. 10.

79. *Science and the Modern World* (New York: Macmillan, 1925), p. 201.

80. Cf. *Experience and God*, p. 118.

81. "Response [to Andrew Reck and Robert Neville]," 285–86.

82. Ibid., 286.

83. It deserves to be noted that, although Professor Smith thinks that the classical American pragmatists provide such resources, he is not at all reluctant to criticize them for the ways they themselves contribute to flattening and constricting the scope of reason. For example, he expresses in *Purpose and Thought* his concern whether Dewey's "severely circumscribed conception of knowing and the conclusions it entails does not in the end contribute to a further widening of the gap between what can be discussed critically and what is merely 'emotive' and thus beyond the reach of rational discourse. That he [Dewey] could have vigorously opposed such a consequence is clear enough, but his thought is not without its own touches of the sort of scientism which makes that consequence inevitable" (p. 152; cf. *Reason and God*, p. 102).

84. So, in "Being and Willing," 26, Smith explores the willing situation.

85. Ibid., 24.

86. Ibid.

87. *Experience and God*, p. 38.

88. Vincent Colapietro, "Toward a More Comprehensive Conception of Human Reason," *International Philosophical Quarterly*, 27, No. 3 (September 1987), 281–98.

89. "Being, Immediacy, and Articulation," 602; cf. 603.

90. Ibid., 602.

91. *America's Philosophical Vision*, p. 41.

92. *Experience and God*, p. 6.

93. *America's Philosophical Vision*, p. 92; cf. p. 93.

94. See, for example, *Experience and God*, p. 38.

95. See, for example, *America's Philosophical Vision*, p. 42.

96. Ibid.

97. Ibid., p. 109.

98. Ibid., p. 112.

99. Cf. *Collected Papers of Charles Sanders Peirce I–V1*, ed. Charles Hartshorne and Paul Weiss (Cambridge, Mass.: The Belknap Press of Harvard University Press, 1931–1935), 5:440.

100. *America's Philosophical Vision*, p. 107; cf. pp. 40, 42.

101. "Being, Immediacy, and Articulation," 594; emphasis omitted.

102. Ibid.

103. Ibid., 596.

104. Ibid.

105. *Experience and God*, p. 111; cf. *America's Philosophical Vision*, pp. 170, 45, 118.

106. See, for example, *America's Philosophical Vision*, p. 39.

107. *Reason and God*, p. 112.

108. Ibid., pp. 107ff.; *Purpose and Thought*, pp. 154ff.; cf. Dewey, "The Subject Matter of Philosophical Inquiry," *Journal of Philosophy*, 12 (1915), 337–45.

109. Smith, *Reason and God*, p. 112.

110. *Experience and God*, p. 113.

111. Ibid.

112. Ralph Waldo Emerson, *Emerson in His Journals*, ed. Joel Porte (Cambride, Mass.: The Belknap Press of Harvard University Press, 1982), p. 452.

John E. Smith and Metaphysics

ROBERT C. NEVILLE

Boston University

THE SPEED-READER flashing through the books and articles of John Smith is likely to be discouraged about finding a metaphysical system. His early work, say up through *Reason and God* (1961), displays two large families of philosophic reference texts.[1] One is the tradition of American philosophy from Jonathan Edwards to the present, as particularly focused in the pragmatists. The other is the tradition of German idealism arising out of Kant and Hegel and focused in the theology of Paul Tillich, with that tradition's particular appropriation of the classical ideas of philosophy and theology in Plato, Aristotle, the Cappadocians, Augustine, and Anselm. The problematics of metaphysics are far more prominent in the latter, idealistic, reference texts than in those of pragmatism.[2] Yet in his later writings the texts of the American tradition have become more and more prominent and those of the European tradition have slipped into subsidiary roles such as providing the context for Royce's thought or expressing positions refuted or improved upon by the Americans. Therefore his later writings seem not to have been framed in the problematics usually associated with metaphysics.

Some adventitious elements might help to understand this shift. In his early period his teaching load, and hence to some degree his research interests, were determined largely by others. So, despite the fact that his dissertation was on Royce, his job at Yale was significantly determined by the need to teach Kant and Hegel. As his student in those days, as both an undergraduate and a graduate student, I took four of his courses on Kant and three on Hegel, which was marvelous for me but probably boring for him.[3] Gaining seniority and powers of academic self-determination, Smith could focus more on his heart's true interests which obviously were in American philosophy.

But the conditions for his placing of the American tradition in the central position were not all adventitious. On the non-postmodern supposition that his own interpretation of the development of his thought has some standing, it is helpful to consult his 1980 essay "Experience and the Boundary between Philosophy and Religion," which is an autobiographical essay in the series *Philosophers on Their Own Work*.[4] He wrote there:

> For a long time I shared with Tillich and many others the belief that one could accept the Kantian theory of human thought and his conclusions *vis-à-vis* metaphysics, while somehow still preserving the metaphysical questions for treatment in some other way.[5]

But after reading Hegel and some of the American philosophers, he said, "I began to think that things need not have stopped with Kant and that the metaphysical and religious questions could still be pursued rationally, but with far more attention to experience and less appeal to the older rationalistic approach."[6]

In the American philosophers he found a conception of experience that had reason, the logos of metaphysics, internal to it rather than in contrast to it. Furthermore, in opposition to the European traditions that take experience to be subjective, he said,

> Once the intuitive certainty of the internal is abandoned, the way is prepared for understanding experience as the medium for the disclosure of a reality which enjoys a tenure beyond the experiencing subject. A long standing bias is reversed: instead of the world "taking place" in "experience," experience takes place in the world. . . . [7]

In Smith's reconstructed sense, experience is less an epistemological category than an alternative to the Aristotelian naturalistic category of causation that connects us with distant things that are as real as we are. But experience has a more direct metaphysical bearing in Smith's thought because, as he also wrote in the same article from which I have been quoting, he has proposed "that experience might serve as a firmament for theology in much the same way as Being had for so many centuries."[8]

With reference, finally, to theology and to the problem of God, we can see now where Smith's metaphysics is to be found. "The God," he said, "who can appear to the religious consciousness as the first certainty becomes, for speculative philosophy, the ultimate problem."[9] "Speculative Philosophy"is the term Smith often uses for metaphysics. Whether he is discussing European or American philosophy, the most prominent problem for Smith has been the problem of God. Knowing that, for him, the concept of experience takes the place of the concept of being in dealing with the problem of God, we can reread his many discussions of experience as metaphysical analyses self-consciously designed to contribute to a speculative understanding of God, as the concept of being was used for that purpose in Tillich and earlier thinkers.

Many philosophers have written about Smith's treatment of experience, none more clearly or eloquently than he himself.[10] My purpose here is not to treat experience *per se* but to reread Smith's theory of experience as a metaphysics. To do this I shall take up two classical metaphysical topics and suggest how his theory of experience addresses them. These topics are: being and God.

Let me admit right away that this procedure does some violence to Smith's thought, because if he had wanted to express himself this way, he would have. He could have written essays and books on systematic topics. Instead he has resolutely chosen the way of commentary. Even the early *Reason and God*, which has some topical chapter titles, is commentarial in its treatment of these topics. Nevertheless, in his commentaries, especially in his interpretations of American philosophy, he has frequently lifted up the dimension of speculative philosophy or metaphysics, restating the thinkers' views so as to set them in the larger context of the Western metaphysical tradition. One remembers his discussions of value, truth, nature, reality, freedom, will, and the Absolute in Royce and the pragmatists, and his consistent criticism of the classical or Humean notion of experience as a metaphysical mistake rather than an epistemological one.[11] So my procedure is a familiar one, except that his are the texts on which I shall comment in ways that set them in the speculative traditions of the West.

BEING

To begin with the question of being: it should first be said that Smith does not equate being and experience. Rather, he has said, as quoted above, that experience plays the role of "firmament" for theology much the way being had. Postponing the relation of experience to theology for the moment, we still can ask how experience relates to being. I believe Smith's position is that being is the capability to enter into experience. This puts him roughly in the tradition of Plato, who defined being as the power to affect another (*Sophist* 247), rather than of Aristotle, who defined being in terms of how a thing has or is its properties, accidentally or essentially (*Metaphysics* V, 7).

For Smith, things enter experience either as subjects experiencing and communicating with each other or as things experienced as interacting with each other. Experience itself is an interaction or transaction, to use Dewey's term as Smith does. Experience is thus one or several of the kinds of interactions in the world and can be understood as such self-referentially. Not all the interactions we experience are themselves experiential interactions; mechanical movements are cases in point. But their being consists in their capacity to enter into experience should an experiencing community or person be at hand. Smith's theory of experience would agree briefly with Kant's that what cannot enter into experience cannot be known. Smith would go further than Kant and say that what cannot enter into experience in principle cannot be real in any significant sense. But he would depart from Kant by claiming that whatever can be conceived can be conceived to be capable of entering into experience; in principle unexperiencable things-in-themselves or unobjectifiable acts of practical reason are inconceivable on Smith's view because his theory of experience allows mediated or indirect access to anything that can be conceived.[12]

That something can be conceived does not, of course, mean that it is real or that it would be experienced if the conditions were appropriate. Some, indeed many, conceivable things are not real. The question whether something is real, however, can be rephrased as the question whether it might truly enter, directly or indirectly, immediately or with mediation, into experience. Its entrance might be actual, potential, or, as Smith is so fond of analyzing, ideal. Smith takes from Peirce the insistence that experience, used in this reconstructed sense, is subjunctive: a thing is capable of entering experience if it would enter experience under the appropriate experiential conditions.

Another metaphysical way of making that point about being is to say that, for Smith, capability of entrance into experience is the "first object of intellect." No matter what things are, or what they do, or how they might enter directly or indirectly, immediately or mediately into experience, to be an object of thought at all a thing must be capable of entering experience.

GOD

When Smith suggests that experience plays something like the role that being used to play in theology, he has in mind the following point. From the credal Trinitarian controversies over *ousia* in Christianity through the scholastic period, being was the concept according to which theologians both distinguished and related God and the world. This was so across many theologies that otherwise were different from one another, even in their interpretations of being. For Smith, the concept of experience functions so as to distinguish and connect God and the world. The analogy goes little further. Smith does not mean that God is pure experience, as many theologians had claimed God is pure being. Nor does he claim with Hartshorne that humans experience imperfectly whereas God experiences perfectly.[13] Rather, God is to be understood relative to the world according to the structures of experience.

From early in his career, Smith has maintained the position expressed in the line quoted above, that "the God who can appear to the religious consciousness as the first certainty becomes, for speculative philosophy, the ultimate problem." The first side of that position has to do with the certainty of God in the religious consciousness. By acknowledging the presence of certainty in the religious consciousness, Smith sets himself over against Hume's tradition of philosophy of religion, according to which God needs to be inferred out of experiential elements. For Smith, as for the entire tradition of *fides quaerens intellectum* he so often cites, inference is always in the middle of experience, never at stages of initial premisses, and for the religious consciousness that experience can

include the certainty of God. Therefore, the question for the religious consciousness is how to understand the experience of God
at hand. Of course, understanding can lead one to believe things
quite opposite to what one believed before, and certainty of God
can be lost. Nevertheless, the certainty of God is both the assumption and the context for the thinking religious consciousness.

In this respect, the theory of experience is what provides the
rationale for understanding how certainty of the Divine "works"
in human life. Smith directs his theory to the distinction between
immediate and direct experience. Immediate experience would be
unmediated by any signs. If we had any truly immediate experience, we would not know we had it; a truly immediate experience
of God could not be distinguished from any other truly immediate
experience. Direct experience, however, engages the object in mutual translations but guides the engagement with signs that can
be corrected through the engagement itself. This is the basic point
of pragmatism, from Peirce on, which Smith has articulated in
such diverse ways.[14] God is present in experience in ways metaphysics might explain; but the grasp of God in experience comes
through the use of signs framed by religion and corrected through
the funded wisdom of the race. Though the signs are fallible, and
hence our minds might be changed about what we are experiencing, the religious consciousness can take God to be more certain
than any of the other fallible interpretations with which experience
is occupied. That is, the religious consciousness can take God to
be the presupposition of all interpretations within experience.[15]

This moves the discussion to the other side of Smith's position
about God: namely, that God is, for speculative philosophy, the
ultimate problem. How do we understand metaphysically that
which experience engages as its most basic presupposition? Smith
is fond of Tillich's theme that God is the presupposition of every
polar distinction in which two different things engage and interde-
fine each other—the distinction, for instance, between subject and
object or self and world. Tillich's neatest expression of this is in
his essay "The Two Types of Philosophy of Religion," but the
theme is developed throughout his writings, particularly in the
Systematic Philosophy.[16]

Tillich's use of polarities is not finally adequate for Smith, however. The subject–object distinction is too deeply rooted in the

European tradition which pragmatism has undermined. Distinctions between subject and object might emerge out of experiential processes, as Peirce and Dewey argued, but the processes of experiential transaction are more basic. God must be understood as a presupposition for experience in a more complicated sense.

Smith is clear that the idea of "religious experience" is not helpful, where "religious experience" means some special experience that alleges to have God as its object.[17] Edwards had refuted the idea of certainty in religious experience long before Schleiermacher and James formulated it.[18] Rather, God is to be understood by speculative philosophy through an analysis of the religious dimension of experience.

Two ideas are especially important for Smith's analysis of the religious dimension of experience.[19] The first is the distinction between the Holy and the Profane. Not all dimensions of life are holy; many aspects of life are properly profane and are to be understood on their own terms. But some events in life, those that push and break the boundaries—such as birth and death, attaining to responsibility, sickness and social tragedy—cannot be dealt with in profane terms and are to be understood as holy. Smith's second idea for understanding the religious dimension is that the holy occasions raise the question of the ground and goal of human life. By this Smith means not merely our causes and purposes, but the ground of the contingent world as such, the purpose of human life as such. The religious dimension of life has to do with acknowledging grounds and affirming purposes of life in the context of the holy.

Whereas Tillich would have said that because we exist there must be a divine ground and because we have ultimate concerns there must be divine purpose, Smith acknowledges the fact that all this is a question. Perhaps life is experienced as non-contingent, or perhaps as nihilistic and empty. Perhaps there are only arbitrary purposes, no human purpose. The experience of our time is filled with precisely these ambiguities. But the religious dimension of experience is the medium, for Smith, through which God can be revealed as ground and goal. Whether God in fact comes through the medium of the religious dimension of experience is an experiential question. Thus Smith is ultimately empirical about God, eschewing the transcendental instincts of the idealists.

Empirically, many people do not experience God, or an equivalent "religious object," and thus their experience is no testimony. On the other hand, many people do experience God as their ground and goal. Their experience is shaped by the symbols and practices of their religious traditions, and by their critiques and rebellions, and thus is fallible. But, given Smith's theory of the religious dimension of experience, no one can argue that the people who experience God as ground and goal are under illusions in so doing. Their experience is as positively justified as any other positive experience, and as fallible as any other positive interpretation. For those to whom God is directly present, their experience is ultimately conditioned by groundedness and purpose. Within the fundamental sense of ground and purpose, all other experiential enjoyments and actions take place. Those without the direct presence of God do not assume groundedness and ultimate purpose. The religious question is not whether the contextualizing assumption of groundedness and purpose is right about experience—both it and its absence are real forms of experience. The religious question is whether God enters experience through the religious dimension to provide groundedness and purpose. Thus Smith holds finally that the question of God is one of revelation, although he rarely uses that word because of its narrow appropriation by the Barthians.

The speculative question of the nature of God, then, turns on the empirical question of what, if anything, comes through the religious dimension. Smith does not, like Whitehead, Hartshorne, or Weiss, attempt to provide a speculative metaphysical model of God that shows what God must be in order to be directly engaged with human experience through the religious dimension. Rather, he describes God in terms of the effects of the encounter with the divine on human experience. I have used here the language of ground and goal, which he developed in *Experience and God*; there are many other expressions, often discussed in commentary on other thinkers.

That Smith declines to describe God in terms of metaphysical categories does not mean that he denies that the question of God is a metaphysical one. On the contrary, he affirms, as quoted twice now, that the metaphysical description of God is the ultimate speculative problem. It remains a problem precisely because a metaphysical theology would have to be derived from an analysis of the direct religiously relevant content of experience. Precisely because that content is mediated by the religious traditions, the metaphysical description of God needs to take the form, at least at the beginning, of commentary on the history of metaphysical theologies East and West.

This returns the discussion to the earlier point: namely, that the idea of experience functions like the idea of being in theology. The idea of being was used to draw the connections and dissimilarities between God and the world, and Smith does so use the idea of experience. He does not define God as the first or last in a chain of profane causes, or as the biggest and best of purposes. Rather, he defines God as that which can come through the religious dimension of experience as the holy ground and goal, providing experience with groundedness and ultimate purpose. Ground and goal themselves can be considered profane terms. What makes them signs of the divine is their location in the transfiguring holiness of the religious dimension of experience. Although not everyone experiences God as ground and goal, those who do are more certain about that, in whatever terms the point is expressed, than about anything else in experience.

I can summarize this brief discussion by saying the John Smith is not a systematic metaphysician in the style of Hegel, Whitehead, or even Tillich. Moreover, if he had wanted to be, he could have been, and, if he changes his mind, still can be. It is an interesting question, which perhaps he will address, whether he believes that the setting forth of a large-scale metaphysical hypothesis would necessarily betray his deep empiricism, in the reconstructed sense of empiricism. That he declines a metaphysical system does not mean that he has no metaphysical position. On the contrary, by means of his elaborate discussion of experience, he has a doctrine of being and a doctrine of God.

I would like to raise one final point, with retrospective and prospective sides. Retrospectively, Smith's own literary career illustrates the displacement of metaphysics from the transcendental mode of idealism to the empirical mode of his reconstructed sense of experience. The groundwork for this was laid by Peirce's theory of hypothesis and Whitehead's treatment of all metaphysical theories, including Descartes's, Leibnitz's, and his own, as hypotheses looking for empirical plausibility. Smith has pushed this move to empirical metaphysics very far indeed.

The prospective part of my point is that, for him, philosophers in the West have not yet absorbed the basic kinds of experience relevant for the parsing of being and God. For instance, experience as shaped in the Indian and particularly Chinese traditions has yet to become familiar to us. Therefore, the full story of Smith's relocation of metaphysics in experience awaits his explorations of the sophisticated philosophies other than those of the Western tradition. His recent discussions of Confucianism are as much a part of his commentarial approach to metaphysics as his early discussions of Royce and Kant.[20]

NOTES

1. *Reason and God: Encounters of Philosophy with Religion* (New Haven, Conn.: Yale University Press, 1961). His first book was *Royce's Social Infinite: The Community of Interpretation* (New York: Liberal Arts Press, 1950). Perhaps *The Spirit of American Philosophy* (New York: Oxford University Press, 1963) ought to be included as "early work"; the point in the text above is relevant to it, and its difference from his later work is indicated in the addition to its revised edition (Albany: State University of New York Press, 1983).

2. Compare, for instance, the treatment of community in the early Royce book with the treatment of the same theme in *America's Philosophic Vision* (Chicago: The University of Chicago Press, 1992), Part II, or even in *Themes in American Philosophy: Purpose, Experience, and Community* (New York: Harper & Row, 1970).

3. At least my vacant face must have bored him. Teaching Kant and Hegel over and over is itself a good thing. From 1965 to 1971 I taught Kemp-Smith's abridgment of the *Critique of Pure Reason* eleven times to freshmen at Fordham in an introductory course that also featured Plato's *Republic*, Descartes's *Meditations*, and Whitehead's *Science and the Modern World*. Good old days?

4. Ed. André Mercier, Fédération Internationale des Sociétés de Philosophie (Bern: Peter Lang, 1980), pp. 191–237.

5. Ibid., p. 196.

6. Ibid.

7. Ibid., p. 199.

8. Ibid., p. 202.

9. Ibid., p. 207.

10. See the other essays on Smith's thought in this volume, all of which treat his experience. See also my essays, "John E. Smith as Jeremiah," *Transactions of the Charles S. Peirce Society*, 22, No. 3 (Summer 1986), pp. 258–71; "On the Relation of Christian to Other Philosophies," in *Being and Truth*, ed. Alistair Kee and Eugene T. Long (London: SCM Press, 1986), and the contribution to the *Festschrift* for Smith, *The Recovery of Philosophy*, ed. Thomas P. Kasulis and Robert C. Neville (Albany: State University of New York Press, 1997). For Smith's own eloquent capsule summary of his theory of experience, see his 1967 Aquinas Lecture, *Religion and Empiricism* (Milwaukee: Marquette University Press, 1967).

11. In addition to *Royce's Social Infinite, The Spirit of American Philosophy, Themes in American Philosophy*, and *America's Philosophic Vision*, which I have already mentioned, see his *Purpose and Thought: The Meaning of Pragmatism* (New Haven, Conn.: Yale University Press, 1978), *Jonathan Edwards: Puritan, Preacher, Philosopher* (Notre Dame, Ind.: University of Notre Dame Press, 1992), and the wonderfully informative Introduction to Jonathan Edwards's *Religious Affections*, The Works of Jonathan Edwards 2 (New Haven, Conn.: Yale University Press, 1959), which Smith himself edited.

12. See *Experience and God* (New York: Oxford University Press, 1968; repr. New York: Fordham University Press, 1995), chaps. 1–3; and *Religion and Empiricism*.

13. See Hartshorne's "Three Strata of Meaning in Religious Discourse," *The Logic of Perfection and Other Essays* (LaSalle, Ill.: Open Court, 1962), and Smith's "Neoclassical Metaphysics and the History of Philosophy," in *The Philosophy of Charles Hartshorne*, ed. Lewis Edwin Hahn, The Library of Living Philosophers 20 (Chicago and LaSalle, Ill.: Open Court, 1991), pp. 498–507.

14. See, for instance, *Purpose and Thought*, chap. 4.

15. See *Experience and God*, chap. 3.

16. "The Two Types of Philosophy of Religion" is the second chapter of *Theology of Culture*, ed. Robert C. Kimball (New York: Oxford University Press, 1959).

17. *Experience and God*, chap. 2.

18. See Smith's *Jonathan Edwards*, chap. 3.

19. See *Experience and God*, chap. 2.

20. See his "Mediation, Conflict, and Creative Diversity," in *Harmony and Strife: Contemporary Perspectives East and West*, ed. Shu-hsien Liu and Robert E. Allison (Hong Kong: The Chinese University Press, 1988), pp. 31–48.

RESPONSES

I WOULD like to begin by expressing my appreciation to those who invested the reading and the thought necessary for the writing of these perceptive papers, to those who arranged the program, and to the audience who were kind enough to come and take part. There is a definite sense in which we come to understand more clearly and precisely what we are saying when we have the response of our readers, which means what they understand us to be saying. I am sure we have all had the experience of saying to a person who has responded to something we have written, "Oh, that is what you think I mean," a remark that points in two directions at once. It suggests, on the one hand, that we think we have been misunderstood, and, on the other, that we had better take a second look at what we have written to see whether our interpreter may have been right and then the question is, "Do I still want to say that?" This experience further confirms what has come to be called the social theory of self-consciousness. On this view we come to know ourselves, the meaning of our experience. and the ideas we are seeking to express, not immediately or intuitively in Cartesian fashion, but through communication with other persons in a continuing dialogue.

J.E.S.

Experience and Its Religious Dimension: Response to Vincent G. Potter

POTTER RAISES A NUMBER of important questions about my interpretation of religion, especially as set forth in *Experience and God*.[1] At the outset, he rightly underlines my basic point that to understand the place of experience in religion we must think in terms of the rich conception of experience developed by Peirce, James, Royce, and Dewey as opposed to the conception of experience to be found in the writings of the British empiricists. To identify experience with the domain of sense, as Locke and Hume did, leads to the exclusion of much that we actually encounter in the world and in ourselves. On the basis of the empiricist view, much of our widespread experience would have to be denied, declared purely subjective or even meaningless. In view of that consequence, it is time to get rid of the theory in order to save the experience. As Potter rightly points out, according to the classical empiricists, experience is a tissue of subjectivity, a veil standing between us and the "external" world, with the result that what we experience is only our own ideas. This view was responsible for the erroneous idea that an item becomes "merely subjective" in virtue of the fact that it enters into experience. Potter gives an admirable account (pp. 9ff.) of what each of the pragmatists contributed to the overthrow of the classical conception of experience and to the formation of the new view.

Potter introduces the important topic of the connection between experience and cognition, and this calls for comment since Locke and Kant identified the two, while Dewey wanted to distinguish between them. Potter cites my distinction between the *cognitive* and the *conative* aspects of experience and of religious faith set forth in *Experience and God*,[2] and, since I used this distinction in a slightly different connection from the one Potter is underlining,

I must clarify the point. The context for my cognitive/conative distinction was a consideration of the force of doubt in religion; I identified the significant content of a religious idea or doctrine with the cognitive, and the person's commitment to or trust in the content with the conative. My chief point was to insist that in addition to cognitive doubt, there can be forms of conative doubt or a weakening of a person's trust and commitment which is *not* necessarily dispelled by arguments and rational considerations appropriate for overcoming doubt on its cognitive side.

I agree with Potter when he says that he does not confine the term "experience" to the cognitive (p. 9), but I believe we are at one in maintaining that there is cognitive experience and that knowledge can arise from experience. The problem was focused in modern philosophy, first, by Kant's equating of experience (*Erfahrung*) and knowledge (*empirische Erkenntnis*) and, later, by Locke and Hume who construed experience in terms of what it would have to be like in order to serve as a basis for knowledge. The case of Kant is most instructive; his taking of experience as theoretical knowledge prevented him from using the expression "moral experience" which would have served to identify the existent morality, or "common moral consciousness," whose principle he sought to formulate. Dewey took note of the problem and sought to resolve it with his distinction between "having" and "knowing." The former stands for what we undergo or participate in directly and which, according to his view, does not need to be known. The latter means the explicit outcome of inquiry conducted in accordance with a logical pattern. I have no objection to this distinction as it stands, but I am concerned about the relation between having and knowing. First, it seems to rule out our "knowing" what we encounter or undergo directly, whether it be the awareness of the splendor of a sunset or more subtle experiences such as expressing gratitude or feeling guilt. In those cases, what fills our consciousness is obviously not the outcome of a controlled inquiry and hence would not qualify as knowledge. Put the other way around: if knowing is excluded from having, the only knowledge we have is theoretical science. I cannot accept that consequence, because the theoretical standpoint, important as it is, is but one among others when we consider the whole spectrum of experience. Making science the final arbiter of knowledge, moreover, has the disadvantage of forcing the religious, the moral, and the aesthetic beyond the bounds of rational discussion. This need not happen, however, if we see that it is philosophy not science which is most appropriate for interpreting and relating all three.

What is needed is not a knife-edge distinction, one that invariably means a separation, but rather a spectrum of knowing, embracing at one end all that we directly encounter and undergo and at the other end the outcome of controlled inquiry. These two ends should not be set in opposition to each other, because conceiving, inferring, appealing to past experience and habitual responses are involved in both. Great confusion results from taking direct undergoing as totally *immediate* and the outcome of inquiry as *mediated*. James's distinction between knowledge by acquaintance and knowledge about, which is clearly akin to Dewey's having and knowing distinction, helps to throw light on the matter. As James pointed out, the two kinds of knowing are clearly reflected in the existence of two terms for "know" in a number of languages. *Noscere, kennen, connaître* mean being acquainted with or familiar with their objects, while their counterparts, *scire, wissen,* and *savoir* mean having theoretical knowledge or information about their objects. I see no reason to deny that acquaintance is a kind of knowledge, but I also see no reason to give it preference as James did when he demoted knowledge about to a "second-hand" status. Experience embraces both kinds of knowledge; much of what we know requires acquaintance, as when we know that honey is sweet only by tasting it, or what awe means by coming into the presence of the Holy, and much of what we know is the result of controlled inquiry under the guidance of an hypothesis. Far from being at odds, the two forms often interpenetrate, so that, for example, in both art and religion, knowing about can enhance and deepen our understanding of what we have experienced directly. Potter catches this point exactly when he writes, ". . . upon reflection what was undergone may demand a cognitive approach [which I take to mean "knowing about"] for the purpose of understanding those experiences" (p. 9).

Potter expresses very well what I mean by the religious dimension of experience when he calls it a context and not a determining *differentia*. The recognition of different contexts of experience identified by a dominant interest, concern, or purpose is one of the distinctive features of the reconstructed conception of experience. Thus we can speak of the moral, aesthetic, religious, political, etc., contexts which represent so many ways in which persons, objects, situations may be *taken* or regarded. A tree on a hillside, for example, may be classified as a botanical specimen in the context of science; it may be appreciated as a synthesis of form and color in the aesthetic context; it may be estimated to be worth so many board feet of lumber in the context of economics. The tree is experienced as having all these dimensions, and it will not do to regard the "real" tree as "nothing but" any one of them alone. The recognition of a multifaceted world reflected in the numerous contexts of experience carries with it an imperative to respect their autonomy but also to seek to relate them to each other which, in turn, requires that we understand what sort of meaning each context is fitted to express. What makes the religious dimension of experience "religious" is the concern manifest in it for the individual's ultimate destiny and purpose, the concern, in short, for God. Since I take the religious dimension to be *generic*, in the sense that it cuts across all religions, the emphasis I place on the disclosure of God (or whatever is taken to be the Holy) is meant to account for a *particular* religious apprehension preserved in an historical religious community and tradition. Both features are necessary; on the one hand, the distinctiveness of the individual religions must not be lost, and, on the other, religion is to be understood as a generic trait of human existence and not, as nominalism would have it, merely a collective name for the many religions that exist. Potter's "experiencing the world religiously" expresses very well in other terms what I mean by the religious dimension. I admit that the expression is somewhat clumsy, but I resort to it as a way of avoiding "religious experience," because I believe that expression has two distinct disadvantages. First, many people equate religious experience with mysticism and that is unfortunate, because the mystical is but one type of religious consciousness.[3] Second is the mistake of taking religious experience in an abstract sense as a *datum* from which to infer the existence of God as its cause. Dewey rightly warned against this idea in *A Common Faith*, but I note that in a recent textbook setting forth the familiar theistic arguments there is an added category called the "argument from religious experience." And, to make matters worse, the author tells us that Peirce's "Neglected Argument" fits into this category. I cannot attempt to correct this misinterpretation here; suffice it to say that Peirce was not proposing to infer the existence of God as the cause of the hypothesis about God's arising from musement on the universes and their relations to each other. Here Potter's "experiencing the world religiously" puts things in the proper perspective: all that we experience takes on a new and deeper meaning when apprehended in relation to God. The phrase "in relation to God" is of the utmost importance, as Potter rightly notes (p. 12) when he stresses my point that the question of the purpose of existence itself—the properly religious question—is also the question of God. Without this connection, the experiential approach collapses into a psychological account in which there is no transcendence.[4]

In *Experience and God* I discussed at some length the way in which the idea of God and the quest for God emerge from the experience of the Holy and the concern for the ground and goal of our being.[5] The main point of that discussion was to throw light on the nature of a particular divine disclosure—revelation in theological language—upon which a particular community and religious tradition have been established. Such a religious community I call "positive religion." Actual disclosure, as we know from the history of religion, has invariably been the culmination of a quest that has found its fulfillment in the discovery of the *concrete* God. It was in this connection that I distinguished between the religious dimension of experience and positive religious faith,[6] and pointed to a *gap* between the two by which I meant that there is "no completely logical transition from the holy as a general category to a definite conception of God such as that found in Christianity."[7] I suggested, however, "that we may begin with the generalized holy as marking out a *possibility* and setting in motion a quest for the concrete God."[8] In considering my account of the special disclosure of God as in the biblical tradition, Potter takes note of my claim that in Christianity, Judaism, and Islam this disclosure was believed to take place not immediately, but only through certain bearers of revelation such as holy persons, historical events, and phenomena of nature. He makes a most important comment about this claim which must command our attention. "I would like to add here on my own account," he writes,

> that when it comes to understanding the conditions of possibility for special disclosure or revelation in holy persons or historical events, disclosure of God in the natural order is first required as a real possibility since without it there would be no way of telling whether what is allegedly disclosed in those persons and events is truly God [p. 13].

What Potter is driving at here is not wholly clear to me, especially the force of "possibility" in both cases, and the reasons for giving priority to the disclosure of God in the natural order and for taking this natural knowledge as a criterion for judging whether the disclosure coming through holy persons and historical events is "truly God." We receive some help in clarifying things from his next two sentences. "I have argued and would argue," he writes, "that some form of 'natural knowledge' of God must be possible if there is to be any 'supernatural revelation.' It seems to me self-evident that in this matter dogmatism is unsatisfactory and an appeal to privileged mystic access is arbitrary." At this point in the discussion Potter directs the reader to an article, "Revelation and 'Natural' Knowledge of God"[9] to which we shall presently turn. First, however, let us consider the clue provided by the last quotation. I take him to be saying that if natural knowledge of God were impossible, any alleged supernatural revelation could be *validated* (is this the meaning of "possible"?) only by a dogmatic insistence or an appeal to mystical insight, neither of which he finds satisfactory.

Is it perhaps the case that Potter's main target here is a position like that of Karl Barth according to which any form of a "natural" theology is ruled out because, apart from the actual revelation, there is no point of "contact" between God and creatures which could serve as a basis for such a theology? God is "wholly other" and reveals Himself only through the divine Word—the Word of Creation in the *Logos* through which all things were made, and the Word of Redemption in Christ. If the Barthian approach is Potter's target here, then I am in agreement with him, although I would state things somewhat differently. I have argued in many places that the revelation to which Barth refers cannot be seen as

merely breaking in upon us without regard for the natural conditions under which alone it could be received and understood by
human beings. These conditions would be the "earthen vessels"
mentioned in the Bible as the only form in which the "Treasure"—
revelation of God—is available to finite human beings. These
"vessels" are the languages and scriptures needed to record the
revelation and the experience of the persons through whom it was
delivered. In addition, there is the need to enlist the resources
of "secular" learning for the translation and interpretation of the
biblical record.

I suspect, however, that Potter means something more by his
appeal to a natural knowledge of God, particularly when he takes
it as a criterion for judging whether what is supposed to be a
"supernatural" revelation is the disclosure of the true God. Hence,
I turn to the article previously noted about revelation and the
natural knowledge of God. I pause to make but one preliminary
point, leaving for later the matter of what relevance it may be said
to have. The point is that Potter uses the distinction, fixed quite
definitely by medieval theologians, between the "natural" and the
"supernatural" knowledge of God, where the former means what
can be known about God through reason and the natural order
(for example, the cosmological arguments for divine existence),
and the latter means a knowledge surpassing human reason contained in divine revelation. I, on the other hand, recast this distinction into one between the order of nature and the historical order.
For biblical religion, the primary medium of divine disclosure
in both Testaments is fundamentally historical, in the sense that
particular historical persons, events, and the pattern manifest in
the course of history itself serve as the bearers of revelation. God,
that is to say, appears in the Bible as speaking to and through
his anointed from Moses to Christ. There is, moreover, a clear
distinction discernible in the biblical writings between the "heavens that declare the glory of the Lord" and the "mighty acts"
through which God made Himself known in history. The reality
of history in biblical religion as the order in which the living God
acts and reveals His will was obscured in the course of the tradition by the tendency to understand the central concept of Being
as fixed, static, and timeless.[10] However, as Hegel and others have

shown, there is no need to think of Being in such restricted terms because of the reality of Becoming.

I stress the point that the special role accorded to history is a *biblical* notion because it might be thought that the idea derives chiefly from those thinkers in the past century who grasped the significance of time, development, and history as keys to the nature of things. We shall return to this topic after considering Potter's article about revelation and the natural knowledge of God.

In his article Potter's central claim is that for revelation to be possible there must be at the least the possibility of a natural knowledge of God, a knowledge, that is, not obtained from revelation; otherwise, there would be no way of knowing that the alleged revelation is from or about God. He goes on to pose two questions which are said to express the cognitive and ontological elements of the problem. The first is whether any religion can consistently claim that there has been a revelation from and about God and at the same time deny that there is any "natural" knowledge of Him. The second is whether any religion can consistently hold that God is the transcendent Creator of the world and at the same time deny that He is immanent. These questions, Potter says, are not new and are important for the religions of revelation, despite the fact that there has not been universal agreement about the answers or even about the precise meaning of the questions themselves. He even suggests that the entire discussion may be due to a verbal misunderstanding, but I believe he is right to dismiss this suggestion in the belief that something substantive is at stake.

My response is that there is indeed something substantive at issue, but that it is complex and involves not one but several questions which might not be framed in the same way in the three traditions. At least one thing is certain: the matter cannot be dealt with on a full scale here. It may, however, be possible to hit upon Potter's central concern so that, despite incompleteness, something of importance will have been achieved.

Before stating what appears to me to be his central concern, I must summarize the four propositions about God and revelation which he believes would be agreed upon by Judaism, Christianity, and Islam. The first is that God is absolutely transcendent and hence neither a finite object nor a collection of all such objects;

the second is that God is the Creator of all finite beings and hence is "near" to them through creative power; the third is that God has revealed Himself in a special way and this revelation has been recorded in a Sacred Book or books; the fourth is that such Revelation must be intelligible to man. In view of these statements, I take it to be Potter's central concern to insist that, in addition to revelation, there is a natural knowledge of God[11] and that without this knowledge we could not know that the alleged revelation is from and about God. Coupled with this concern, if I understand him correctly, is an insistence that a revelation or divine self-disclosure must be intelligible to the human beings to whom it was addressed.

Although I am not entirely clear as to how natural knowledge of God provides a ground for knowing whether revelation is from and about God, I believe I understand what Potter is driving at and, while I would put the matter differently, I am in substantial agreement with him. He is claiming as a necessary condition that the God of revelation and the record through which that Revelation comes to us not be totally other than and discontinuous with (a) the understanding we have of God through nature and (b) the capacity we have to think, experience, and interpret which makes it possible for us to be addressed by a revelation in the first place. I have repeatedly argued against the idea that revelation discloses a God who is "wholly other" and inaccessible to human thought and experience. It is for this reason that I found the anti-philosophical approach of Karl Barth unacceptable, especially by comparison with the correlation method of Paul Tillich which recognizes the essential involvement of theology with "secular" learning and preserves the philosophico-theological dialectic.[12]

I did not mention it sooner because Potter does not dwell on it at length, but in the essay noted above about natural knowledge of God in relation to revelation he does have a brief statement of the view adopted by Aquinas in this regard and that may well give us the key to his own position. He says, referring to the questions noted above, that Aquinas would have held that it is inconsistent to hold for a divine revelation and deny that we have natural knowledge of God, and, further, that an absolutely transcendent God who is also Creator must be immanent in the world.[13] The underlying idea is that unless we have knowledge of God obtained from a source other than revelation we have no way of knowing that the revelation is from and about God. That other source is, presumably, what can be known on the basis of reason and experience about God as immanent in nature. We are now on familiar ground; the natural knowledge of which Potter speaks is the same as the natural theology of Aquinas according to which we can know, apart from revelation, that God exists and that God is one. This is the knowledge that we must have if we are to know whether an alleged revelation is from God. Curiously enough, the point comes through more clearly in Potter's fanciful comparison with the tooth-fairy. "Even to claim to have had a revelation from the tooth-fairy," he writes, "one would have to have some idea of what properties belong to the tooth-fairy and have some reason to believe that there exists a tooth-fairy who could make such a revelation."[14] In short, to talk about a revelation of God at all, it is necessary for us to know, apart from that revelation, that there is a God to be revealed and something at least about the divine nature. The question about whether a revelation is from and about God becomes the question whether the revealed God is the *same* as the God who is the object of natural knowledge. If I am correct in thinking that Potter's position here is the same as that of Aquinas, it will repay us to consider briefly how Aquinas sought to deal with the problem of the same God.

Aquinas's now classical arguments for the existence of God must be accounted "natural" knowledge of God since they represent the operation of reason in its own sphere and apart from revelation. The question may then be raised, as it has been by Copleston and others, whether and in what sense Aquinas was justified in ending each of the five proofs with some such expression as "this (that is, a First Mover, a First Cause) everyone understands to be God." Copleston suggests that even if it is granted that there is a First Mover, a First Cause, and an absolutely necessary being, it does not immediately follow that it is appropriate for this being to be called "God." I agree with Copleston here because the term "God" was surely taken as a name connoting a personal being and not as a generic concept. Copleston appears to have something similar in mind when he says that if we take into account the fourth and fifth arguments leading to the existence of a personal supreme being, "it is true to say that 'all men' call this being 'God,' in the sense that all who acknowledge the existence of a transcendent, supreme and uncaused cause do in fact recognize this being as divine."[15] Copleston goes on to say, however, that these features do not exhaust what is meant by the term "God" which is why he believes that Aquinas's discussion of the divine attributes must be taken together with the proofs. I agree with him on this point, but there is still the question of what is meant by "all men," "everyone," and "we" and what they understand by "God" when they acknowledge that the First Mover, Cause, etc., is God. This question prompts another: Would their understanding of "God" not have to have a content prior to their acknowledging the identity of the First Cause, Mover. etc., and that "God"? About the first question, must we not take into account the fact of the Christian tradition and the idea of the biblical God as informing the minds of the "everyone" who understands that this God is the same as the First Mover, etc.? If this is so, we have a key to answering the second question. The prior understanding of "God" stems from "the God of Abraham, Isaac, and Jacob," and this is essential if we are to avoid a divorce between the biblical God and the so-called "God of the philosophers." Theology would then be the intelligible articulation of the God disclosed in the biblical record—"faith seeking understanding" where "intelligible" means that we are constrained to understand the God of revelation in terms continuous with reason and experience.

This resolution, however, would probably not fulfill Potter's condition that natural knowledge of God derived from the immanence of God in the world is needed if we are to know whether any alleged revelation is from and about God. As I noted previously, it is not clear to me how such knowledge serves as a warrant for revelation. Nevertheless, I would insist on a very basic condition, and I believe that Potter would agree: namely, that the God disclosed in the biblical record as Redeemer cannot be in contradiction to the God who is known from the existence of the world and certain of its features as Creator.

I turn now to Potter's questions about the meaning of the pairs "immediate/mediate" and "direct/indirect." These are important questions, and I shall try to clarify the distinctions and respond to his challenge: Can we have it both ways and, if so, how? I came to adopt the second of the two pairs when I discovered that the "immediate/mediate" dyad omits something important. In denying that any experience of God could be immediate, I mean much the same as Potter does when he says that there must be something connecting the extremes.[16] I understand this to be a medium which I express in the claim that any alleged encounter with God is also an encounter with something else, as we see in the case of Moses and the burning bush and the vision of St. Paul on the road to Damascus. The absolutely immediate is inarticulate; whatever voice it receives comes by way of mediation. I take this to be in accord with Peirce's theory of signs and interpretation, and I believe that Potter and I are together on this point.

The "direct/indirect" dyad is more complicated. I believe, however, that I now have a more adequate way of expressing the point than I had in some earlier writings. My reason for preferring "direct" to "immediate" arises from an analogy between the person-to-person encounter and that of a person and God. I want to say that in meeting you and conversing with you I encounter you directly but not immediately; first, because of the need for signs to communicate, and, second, because it is highly artificial—witness the "other minds" arguments—to say that I *infer* your existence as if I first knew of my own existence and then inferred yours by analogy. Nonetheless, it now seems to me to be going against the facts to exclude inference entirely from what I am calling direct experience, since I have come to see that inference can be understood in a sense that overcomes what has for some time been my main misgiving: namely, that it means a logical transition to what is *absent*, or the invocation of a "must be" that seems less palpable than an "is." The problem has been my failure to take seriously the bearing of the reconstructed conception of experience on the role of inference within its reach. According to the new view, experience has "fringes" and a depth going beyond the central focus of any particular experience. Since inference occurs *within* experience and need not be set in contrast to it as a matter of "reason" as in the dichotomy set up by Locke and Hume, inference need not be to the absent, but rather to what is *present* either at the fringe or in the depth of an encounter. I shall go on to point out the importance of this idea in the succeeding discussion of the arguments for God's reality.

I fully appreciate Potter's perceptive comments about the theistic proofs and I shall attempt to respond to them with what I believe is a better understanding of these arguments and how they might be connected than I had when I wrote *Experience and God*. I have been concerned for some time about whether the two ways of approach to God which find expression in the ontological and the cosmological arguments respectively can be brought into some sort of harmony with each other. To do so is important since, in addition to the differences between the arguments as such, there is also the fact that the two lines of thinking represent two ways of understanding the relation between God and human experience and reflection.

I would like to begin by offering a few general comments about religion, reason, and argument. First, I entirely agree with Potter, as I noted previously, that it is an error to drive a wedge between the God of the philosophers and the God of Abraham, Isaac, and Jacob. I have repeatedly claimed that there is an internal connection between religion with its theological expression and philosophy, and I have sought to show in what ways each suffers from being separated from the other. When religion rejects the goad provided by metaphysical reflection and encapsulates itself within a closed circle, biblical or dogmatic, it positivizes itself and tries to rival science, but with "religious facts" (the claim, for example, that "creation science" should be taught side by side with evolutionary biology), and abandons the ancient effort at "faith seeking understanding" initiated by the Alexandrians and deepened by Augustine and Anselm. Philosophy, on the other hand, in shutting out the goad of religion with its concern for ultimate questions—God, destiny, freedom, evil—likewise positivizes itself, dismisses metaphysical questions as meaningless or due to the misadventures of human speech, and reduces philosophy to analysis and criticism, often with the suggestion that it should give way either to literature or to politics. The mutual involvement of religion and philosophy was the underlying theme of *Reason and God* and stemmed from the belief that Christianity, as a religion committed to the *logos* doctrine that there is a thread of intelligibility running throughout the cosmos, including its relation to the human mind, cannot countenance, as Potter rightly says, the two Gods. The divorce between them—echoed in antiquity by Tertullian's "what has Athens to do with Jerusalem?" reinforced later by Kierkegaard's setting the God of the Patriarchs against Hegel's Absolute Spirit, and finally, by Barth's attempt to construct a purely biblical theology exclusive of philosophy—cannot be consistently maintained. The chief reason is that to set forth the biblical picture of God's nature and relation to the world in a systematic way requires categories and concepts that are not derivative from the Bible, but emerge from pervasive experience and reflection. From the history of Christian theology we learn that those who have rejected the interplay between theology and philosophy have been in the minority and that it is with great difficulty that a clear line can be drawn so as to distinguish between the biblical God and the so-called God of the philosophers.

The second point to be stressed is that rational reflection about God should not ignore or obscure the *religious* significance of the discussion. The remarkable resurrection of the ontological argument some years ago nicely illustrates this point. As Hartshorne noted in his survey of the treatment of the argument by philosophers, that renewal showed no concern for the particular meaning of the concept of God or for its religious significance, since the argument was taken as an occasion for exercises in modal logic and for continuing the argument about whether existence is a predicate. My concern for religious relevance does not mean that I undervalue the logic of the argument. On the contrary, I hold that it contains a valid logical transition, one that is obscured by declaring the argument "self-evident." The transition consists in grasping the point that the "God" who might *not* have been real is *not* identical with the "God" identified through Anselm's formula as "that than which no greater can be conceived."

Rational reflection, to be authentic, must be constrained by the nature of the subject matter under consideration; in the case of religion this means taking into account the total personality of those in whom religious faith finds its life. James was quite vehement in his attack on philosophers who make religion into a wholly intellectual affair and neglect its ethical and aesthetic aspects. I do not disagree; hence along with my emphasis on religious intelligence and understanding I recognize the rights of what James called our "passional nature" and do not suppose that religion finds its life in dialectic alone. There are, in fact, good reasons for holding that arguments for God's reality are late comers on the scene and their appearance may even be a sign that an earlier, instinctive belief has lost its hold. That there are predispositions to belief cannot be denied, but it is not to be supposed that they exist only for believers in God since there are dispositions to disbelief as well. Why, for example, should Bertrand Russell (I cite him only as a symbol, since nothing personal is meant) have been "jubilant," as he said, when he was convinced that the ontological argument is invalid? Do we not have here a predisposition to disbelief which has now been strengthened by the overcoming of a formidable challenge?

I can best conclude this response by making a summary statement about Potter's questions dealing with the difference between the approach through intelligibility and the way of demonstration. In this connection I cannot overemphasize the debt I owe to Tillich's essay "The Two Types of the Philosophy of Religion." It is a brilliant account of the two approaches, the type of rationality involved in each, and the sort of spirituality each expresses. One starts with the *self* and seeks through reflective meditation akin to Platonic dialectic to recover the presence of the Uncreated Light in the depths of the soul. The other starts with the *world* and seeks to demonstrate with an appeal to causality in the fashion of Aristotle that the reality of God follows from the contingent existence of the world.[17] I believe that Potter would agree with me in thinking that both ways are necessary because each does something that the other does not, while having the same end in view. Support for this claim is found in Peirce's critique of the chain model of argument according to which the chain is only as strong as its weakest link and his proposal of the rope analogy where several strands of argument aiming in the same direction lend each other mutual support.

Characteristic of the Augustinian/Platonic way is its focus on the relation between God and the soul; its chief text echoes this relation—"Arise, O my soul, enter the inner chamber of thy mind and shut out all thoughts save that of God alone." Guided by the belief that the "things above us" are to be understood in terms of the signs and likenesses found in the "things below," Augustine pursued his aim of faith seeking understanding. The role of reason is to find this understanding more in *insight* and *meaning* than in formal *demonstration*. Augustine's most extensive effort in this direction is the *De Trinitate* where he sought to understand the relations between the Persons in the triune God after the model of threefold divisions in the soul. The quest for illumination is undergirded by the identification of God with the first principles of *Sapientia*—*Verum, Bonum, Esse*—and the goal is the recovery, through divine illumination, of the *presence* of God in the soul. The reflective process involved is more akin to the Platonic dialectic in which the mind is led to "see" a truth or a meaning than to the syllogistic of Aristotle with its necessary conclusions.

One feature of the Augustinian view—the kind of significance it assigned to the world—turned out to be a major factor in its eclipse at the end of the Middle Ages. It will be recalled that in Augustine's dialogue with Reason in the *Soliloquia*, the question is put, "What is it that you most want to know?" to which Augustine replied, "God and the soul." To the further question, "Nothing else?" he answered, "Absolutely nothing." This subordination of the world was echoed in his concern that natural curiosity about the inner workings of nature would serve only to distract the mind from its proper focus on God. The world for Augustine was not primarily a physical reality, but rather a realm of symbols, similitudes, and signs through which the things of religion are to be understood. It is not difficult to see why this picture of the world could not remain intact after the introduction of Aristotle's natural philosophy and metaphysics into theological thinking by Albert and Aquinas. For Aristotle, the world was a vast dynamic and organic system of genera and species, very palpable indeed because he believed that it was eternal and had no beginning.

Having adopted Aristotle, Aquinas set the stage for a new beginning. The self is no longer the point of departure; the new starting point is the world, including the basic fact of its existence plus some of its generic features such as motion and causal connections between things. With the new starting point also went a new way of understanding God which found expression in the now familiar cosmological proofs for His existence. There are, however, important differences between the meditative quest through the soul for the intelligibility of faith running from Augustine through Anselm to Bonaventure, and Aquinas's program for demonstrating God's existence by invoking causality and the contingency of the world. While I believe there is a way to close the gap between these two approaches, I do not believe the matter can be resolved by pretending that there is no gap at all. I do not claim that Potter holds this view, because he obviously does not, but I would like to cite the words of a highly regarded and influential interpreter of Aquinas who did espouse such a view. In his concise and clearly written monograph *Thomas Aquinas*, Dr. Martin Grabmann states:

> Anselm of Canterbury had inaugurated Scholasticism proper and had pointed to the true essence of the Scholastic method by espousing the program inspired by Augustine: *Credo ut intelligam*—I place myself firmly on the platform of faith in order to penetrate further into the content of faith by means of reason. The ideas of Thomas regarding the function of reason in the service of faith are nothing but a further development of this position. Thomas took up this idea of Anselm, which was transmitted and lived on in the thought of Hugo and Richard of St. Victor, Robert of Melun, Simon of Tournai, and especially William of Auxerre, and formulated it more clearly and explicitly from the standpoint of a better developed conception of faith and knowledge. The emphatic theological idealism and spiritualism of Anselm and the Victorines was conducted into the sober channel of precise and clear concepts.[18]

One need have no quarrel with this statement insofar as it affirms the continuation from Augustine of the general belief that reason can function in the service of faith. To suppose, however, that there is no difference in the way this function was carried out as meditation and dialogue aims at leading the person to "see" with the mind's eye some truth about things; emphasis falls on the person's *participation* in the dialogue which in turn has an effect on his or her life and character. In this sense the approach has an important subjective side. By contrast, Aristotelian reasoning, while it may also be seen as a leading of the mind, is largely objective and impersonal; the conclusion of the argument follows of necessity from the premises and stands there, so to speak, whether any individual affirms it or not. Put in other terms: the difference is between a dialogue of experiential discovery and a logic of deduction. Here, as before, I am led to ask why it should be taken for granted that it is necessary to decide the superiority of one over the other. May we not have both, coupled with an acknowledgment that, given the variety of human experience, we must allow for the varieties of religious experience within the same tradition.

NOTES

1. (New York: Oxford University Press, 1968; repr. Fordham University Press, 1995).

2. Pp. 102ff.

3. I find it helpful in this connection to point out that, for example, neither Christianity nor Islam is *essentially* mystical, but that both have developed forms of mysticism within their respective traditions.

4. *Experience and God*, p. 56.

5. Philosophical interpretation of religion is faced with the perennial problem that it is necessary to have some term designating the supreme object of worship, but one which is not at the same time a *name* for that reality in a particular religion. I have proposed "Religious object" which, although not entirely adequate because the reality is not an "object," is nevertheless a viable alternative to having to take the term "God" as both a name and a concept.

6. *Experience and God*, pp. 68ff.

7. Ibid., pp. 75–76.

8. Ibid., p. 76; emphasis added.

9. In *Neoplatonism and Islamic Thought*, ed. Parvis Morewedge (Albany: State University of New York Press, 1992), pp. 247–57.

10. For many years I have argued in behalf of a philosophical theology and on this account I am critical of the Reformed tradition when it rejects philosophy and insists that the involvement of Christianity with ancient philosophy distorted the original *Kerygma*, thus making it necessary to construct theology from purely biblical sources. My objections to this view were stated above in the text.

11. I think Potter need not qualify his claim so that it includes only the "possibility" of such knowledge; it may be, however, that he wants to object to the idea that, from the standpoint of revelation, natural knowledge of God is ruled out altogether—i.e., is *impossible.*

12. As an example of the gulf Barth insisted upon between the biblical Word and all human thought, we may take his discussion of Nothingness in the thought of Heidegger and Sartre. The care with which he presents their positions leads the reader to expect a comparison between their conceptions of Nothingness and the Nothingness from which God cre-

ated the world in the biblical account. The expectation is disappointed; no comparison occurs because, we are told, the Nothingness of which the philosophers speak could not, in principle, be the same as that of the Bible.

13. "Revelation and 'Natural' Knowledge of God," p. 251.

14. Ibid.

15. F. C. Copleston, *Aquinas* (Harmondsworth: Penguin, 1955), p. 130.

16. I believe that mysticism is a special case and requires a longer treatment than is possible here. If we take as examples the experiences of Bonaventura and Meister Eckhart, it seems clear that the end of their quests—in one case the all-consuming love and in the other the sacred silence—is the immediate, but the path to the goal certainly is not. That path is the negations that must be made in order to prepare the self for the final experience.

17. Anselm brought the ontological way to its fullest expression, and Aquinas gave the cosmological arguments their clearest focus. Anselm, starting with the self meditating on the idea of God, pointed to the logical consequences of understanding God as "that than which nothing greater can be conceived." Aquinas, starting with the existence and some features of the world, sought to demonstrate the reality of God through causality. It has not always been noticed that Descartes confused the picture by starting with the idea of God in the ontological way, but then followed the cosmological way by asking for the *cause* of that idea in a finite mind. That was not Anselm's way, and, in fact, Descartes's hybrid represents neither Anselm nor Aquinas.

18. *Thomas Aquinas: His Personality and Thought*, trans. Virgil Michel, O.S.B. (New York: Longmans, Green, 1928), pp. 91–92.

Morality, Religion, and the Force of Obligation: Response to Robert J. Roth, S.J.

Roth raises a number of important questions prompted by views I have expressed about morality, the nature of moral obligation, and the relations between religion and morality. When I consider responding to his comments and questions, I cannot avoid the sense that I have fallen into a pattern set by William James who was a moralist in his basic outlook on life, but who wrote little specifically about ethics beyond his essay on the moral philosopher and the moral life. I am indebted to Roth for bringing together from a number of places the main points I have sought to make about the moral dimension of experience and our life in the world. He rightly calls attention to the importance I attach to the ideal of self-realization, embracing both individual self-fulfillment and the contribution of individual talent to the well-being of the community. I was first attracted to this ideal by reading Bradley's *Ethical Studies* and later on by Royce's idea that to be is to be the fulfillment of a purpose; in both cases I took special note of their conceptions of the self and of the emphasis placed on self-determination. Roth cites the tension I find in Royce's thought at this point: on one side there is his idea that the individual self is essentially a meaning unified by a dominant purpose or a will defining what the individual *means to be* and on the other is the Absolute whose purpose is fulfilled in the selection of each individual and, while Royce does not use this language, I take it to specify what the individual *is meant to be* in terms of the cosmic purpose. Stated in the simplest terms, the problem is how it is possible for an individual to define itself when, from the standpoint of the Absolute, he or she is already defined. I shall not join this issue here; I bring it up because Roth (pp. 20–21) says that a similar problem exists in connection with my conception of morality. The topic is discussed below.

Roth begins with my article, "Religion and Morality" which he rightly calls an "early" article and later suggests (p. 29) "that Smith would want to modify that position." I entirely agree; the claim I made was far too strong. I took the position that there is no morality without religion and based it on the Christian belief that the "vertical" relation between the individual and God—love—must be the ground of the "horizontal" relation that should obtain between individuals. What I had in mind is found in the First Epistle of John—"If a man say, I love God, and hateth his brother, he is a liar." I agree with Roth that, even if we were sure that this is the basic Christian view, my extending it to the denial that there is morality without religion is too narrow a view and not nearly dialectical enough to deal with all the philosophical issues involved. Moreover, I am surprised in retrospect that I ever thought it a simple matter to hold that morality is both autonomous and yet necessarily rooted in religion. I shall return to the point after briefly offering some reasons why I believe that the two are distinct dimensions of life and yet are related in some intimate way.

To begin with, I insist that the issue is one of principle and that whether morality is independent of religion is not to be decided by citing those who acknowledge moral standards while insisting that they as persons are not "religious." If morality concerns what we *do* and religion what we *are*, then we can ask the question about how *doing* and *being* are connected and seek an answer by an appeal to experience.[1] Roth's comments (p. 20) lead me to understand now what motivated me earlier on: namely, my inability to see how any view of the good life can be set forth which is free of assumptions about the nature of human beings and their destiny in a total scheme of things. The latter I identify with religion, but it is not to be supposed that views about the destiny of human beings are to be found only in the religions proper. In the original paper I cited Dewey's belief that man, through technological prowess, is to control the conditions of his existence, and it is clear that both Nietzsche and Sartre believed that the final destiny of man is to control his own destiny, thus combining self-creation and redemption. The bearing of these quasi-apocalyptic visions on the conception of morality and what it is imperative for human beings to choose is obvious in both cases.

If it seems too paradoxical to call these beliefs by the name of "religion," let us say that they are closely related to the religious concern, since for both thinkers the projection of authentic human existence was meant to replace God. If I understand Roth's point here, he is suggesting that I not settle the matter solely on the basis of the biblical view. I agree with him, not least because there is a wealth of other experience to be taken into account.

Before turning to Roth's searching questions about the origin of moral obligation and what distinguishes the moral from the aesthetic and the intellectual, I would like to bring up another theme that was discussed in the article under consideration: namely, the *tension*, if not antagonism, which can arise between religion and morality and how both are affected by it. Royce pointed out long ago that the much heralded conflict between science and religion is far easier to overcome than the lesser-known confrontation between religion and morality. His point was that whatever discrepancies, real or alleged, there may be between scientific knowledge and religious insight, science is not fitted to take the place of religion in human life, but the same is not true of morality. As we know from the history of religion and from modern secularized society, morality can lay claim to the entire realm of value and worth and thus declare that religion is superfluous. This claim is in fact expressed in the credo of the international Humanist movement; not only is morality independent of religion, but morality is said to be enough. Religion should be abandoned since it is no more than a carryover of superstition in a secular world of science and technology. I cannot join this issue here, but I have discussed it at some length in a recent book, *Quasi-Religions*. I am convinced that no adequate understanding of either morality or religion is possible without coming to terms with what the tension between them means and especially how that tension is being played out in our present situation. It is because the two are near-relations that they are capable of a strife not possible for total strangers, and we see this strife most clearly when each tries to sit in judgment of the other. The voice of religious faith calls the one who absolutizes duty and earnest endeavor in the service of a moral ideal a "mere moralist" who underestimates the force of sin and has no place for a power of grace beyond human striving. From the other side, the champion of duty sees the religious believer as a shirker of responsibility who is ready to take what James called a "moral holiday" because he believes that the power of God has already overcome the dark powers of the world. The moralist is not on good terms with the idea uppermost in the religious mind that we need to be delivered from our capacity for evil, while the religious person sees only pride and vainglory in the idea uppermost in the moral mind that the right and good must be done though the heavens fall. The chief lesson to be learned here is that religion and morality belong together because neither can do the work of the other. A religion without moral obligations would be purely contemplative and aesthetic, an appreciation of the beauty of holiness without duties to others. A morality without religion turns into a graceless moralism and self-righteousness without any sense of a divine power beyond, a power able to temper justice with mercy and law with love. In the light of Roth's criticism and the foregoing considerations, I am now inclined to think that making clear the unique contributions of the two dimensions of experience is more important than an attempt to demonstrate in an abstract way that there can be no morality without religion.

Returning to Roth's questions about the nature and source of moral obligation, I find a cluster of three closely related issues. First, the distinctive nature of moral obligation; second, why one is obliged to seek self-realization; third, the problem of understanding how love can be commanded. To begin with, Roth rightly notes that I include law and obligation in what is essential for morality (p. 22), but that I also express "caution" about them. Although the two are closely related, I would like to consider them separately in order to point out that law is not the only source of obligation and that obligation also figures essentially in a morality based on love which both is and is not a matter of law.

On the first issue, I believe that Kant was correct in holding that the experience of obligation—having the sense of *ought*, being under, or placing oneself under, orders—is unique to human beings and is essential for morality. I would say that his conception of a moral imperative expresses the *form* of morality, in the sense that what we hold before us as an ideal of right and/or good carries with it, if we are to be not *self*-contradictory (in the primordial human meaning of this term before it was assimilated entirely by logic), the obligation to choose and act in accordance with that ideal. One can see the point in a comparison with Mill's utilitarianism, a position intended to be the opposite of Kant's. Mill insisted that the greatest happiness principle does not mean the individual's happiness but the happiness of the greatest number. Does this not imply that the principle *ought* to be followed in situations where an individual cannot readily see that there is "an indissoluble association between his [or her] own happiness and the good of the whole"? In short, even when an individual has no sincere conviction about this indissoluble association between individual happiness and the good of the whole, there remains an obligation to the principle. I do not see how there can be any morality at all without such a constraint.

My "caution" about law in morality stems from the insight that the relation between a person and a law is *external*, in the sense that law represents a norm standing in opposition to the human will. Kant took note of this externality when he claimed that a Holy will would not experience obligation because it already embodies or has internalized the law, whereas it is distinctive of a human, imperfect will that its law confronts it as something commanded and hence as something the will could oppose. Kant, moreover, perceived the shortcoming of law when he saw the need for a mediating motive in action which he found in the special feeling of *respect (Achtung)* for the moral law. This respect springs from but one source, the *thought* that only human beings can experience obligation and are thus capable of self-legislation. Respect does reduce the externality somewhat, but to reduce it further requires a love that goes beyond law, but without at the same time annulling it. I shall return to this point in considering how love can be commanded; in the meantime, I shall go on to Roth's questions about the distinctive character of obligation and its relation to the ideal of self-realization.

I fully agree with Roth that morality includes an obligation that is distinct from an invitation (pp. 22–23), and to say that one *ought* to appreciate a work of art is not ordinarily taken to mean the same sort of thing as when we say that one *ought* to tell the truth. Here I agree that the difference is between aesthetic taste or sensibility and moral sensitivity or character. But this difference itself stands in need of further clarification. The most obvious difference between the two has to do with the exercise of volition and the effort that goes into overt action. In the moral situation we are called upon to choose and act in accordance with a conception of a good to be realized or of the right thing to be done. The underlying assumption is that we have the *power* of choosing and acting, no matter how limited it may be. There is in the aesthetic situation no corresponding demand for action since it is not generally assumed that aesthetic appreciation or taste is something that we command at will. We may on occasion say or feel that others "ought" to appreciate the beauty of a painting we treasure or that they *should* experience as awesome the power of a Niagara Falls. If we do, however, there is no demand for action in either case; the only effort implied in saying "you ought to appreciate . . ." is whatever needs to be done in order to cultivate taste or deepen the experience of artistic creations. To put the point in another way: it makes eminent sense to say that we can experience an obligation to refrain from appropriating what belongs to another, but does anyone actually experience an obligation to appreciate a work of art? The idea seems to me highly artificial.

Closely related to his concern that the moral and aesthetic not be confused, is Roth's charge that in calling law "intelligent design" I am identifying the moral with intelligence (p. 23–24). "Intelligence" is not without ambiguity; it may mean that someone possesses knowledge, is well focused, understands the relevance of information to the problem at hand, and has sound judgment, all of which may be accounted as virtues. These, however, as Plato and Socrates made so clear, may all reside in and determine the behavior of a scoundrel engaged in all sorts of misconduct. On that account alone, intelligence cannot constitute morality as such.[2] I would say that since intelligence is needed for pursuing the ideal of self-realization we have a moral obligation to seek it. Willing such an ideal entails a commitment to determine the most appropriate and morally valid means to achieve it. Intelligence, nevertheless, is no substitute for morality simply because it may be made to serve evil ends.

Perhaps this is the proper place to call attention to a source of misunderstanding about obligation which stems from the tension, and sometimes polar opposition, between the two basic conceptions of morality which have developed in the Western tradition.

I have in mind the well-known distinction between the *good* and the *right*. According to a tradition going back as far as Aristotle, the virtuous life is the realization of human capabilities and talents guided by an end thought to be *good* in itself and not a means to some further end. Aristotle called this good *eudaimonia*, which may be translated as happiness or well-being. The chief emphasis in a morality of the good is on the development and growth of potentialities in accordance with virtue. The second tradition, often associated with the Stoics in antiquity and with Kant's ethics in the modern world, insists that morality is defined by what is *right* and expressed in a law or principle—that truth be told, that justice be done—which it is the duty of each person to uphold.

Consideration of the strengths and weaknesses of these two theories of morality is not possible here; I believe, however, that neither position is entirely adequate and that we need both since each focuses on an essential feature that is subordinated in the other. The misunderstanding I referred to above comes about because the ideal of self-realization defines a morality of the good, and critics of the position have claimed that it is lacking in obligatory force. I am attempting to combine the two positions, specifying self-realization as the *good* to be pursued, and claiming that we are obligated by principles which are derived from the *right* and determine how the self realizes itself in relation to others in a moral order.

I suspect that it is because the morality of the good underemphasizes obligation that Roth asks why one is "*morally* obliged" to seek the full development of the self. The direct answer is that, if self-realization is put forward as the good, the moral obligation to pursue it follows. I am, however, hesitant to leave the matter there because something important is being left out: namely, the appropriateness of "why" questions about the foundations of morality. I am uneasy about such questions because they inevitably slide into the notorious question, "Why should I be moral?" Just raising this question implies a demand for some guarantee that a further good will be forthcoming as the incentive (reward?) for obedience to moral principle. Morality, in short, is made into a means so that virtue is no longer its own reward. I shall assume that Roth is not asking the question I find dubious, but is looking instead for some deeper source of moral obligation than can be found in any utilitarian justification.

The main reason why obligation does not loom large in a self-realization morality is that each of us has a "natural" tendency in that direction. Kant noted this fact when he claimed that the pursuit of happiness is not a genuine duty because it is something I would attempt to do in any case as a human being and quite apart from any moral law or obligation. There are, however, further considerations to be taken into account. The self to be realized is the good or higher self, the self of creative and constructive capabilities, the self who is obliged to act in accordance with moral principle. There are two sides to the equation: on the one side is the self who pursues a vocation or a unifying purpose and practice; and, on the other, the manner in which the pursuit of the goal takes place. The task is to decide, through all the avenues of self-examination and knowledge, what self we are best fitted to realize, and then follows the obligation to realize ourselves in a way that is compatible with the realization of other selves in a moral community. This means that I do not make my way by cheating my neighbor, deceiving my friends, sacrificing truth to appearance and expediencies, and treating others as if they were objects to be used and not persons.

I am under no illusions about the difficulty we face in finding our vocation or the self that is to be realized, but I believe it is possible to steer a middle course between the extremes of projecting ourselves in total freedom out of nothing and of accepting a previously determined self defined essentially by "my station and its duties." The meaning of these alternatives will become clearer if we consider briefly how they developed in modern thought. Kant began a new line of thinking when he questioned the traditional idea of the self as a substance—whether the rational animal of Greek thought or the *res cogitans* of Descartes—with a fixed nature, already "there" at the outset, which unfolds in the course of time. Instead Kant declared that, unlike objects which do have a determinate "nature," human beings have the capacity of building a moral *character* through the exercise of freedom. A character is analogous to a nature, but it is not given in advance and is not like a permanent possession because it must be willed (self-determination) ever anew, which means that I must continue to choose that character. Kant was thus moving in the direction of identifying the self with freedom, but he did not go as far down that road as Nietzsche and Sartre were to go more than a century later. Kant sought to maintain a balance between freedom and destiny by distinguishing between what Nature makes of man and what man makes of himself. Each individual inherits or is determined by past historical and cultural factors over which he or she had no control, to say nothing of a biological inheritance that constitutes in a literal sense a natural endowment beyond the power of human freedom. According to Kant, however, there is within our power the freedom to shape the moral contours of our life and form consistency of character. Thus justice is done to the fact that by the time we reach the age when informed choice is possible, our life and situation have already been determined in many significant respects and without our consent; at the same time room is left for the exercise of our freedom within these limits. I find this balanced position, based as it is on the idea of freedom rather than the traditional notion of substance, more realistic and in accord with experience than the belief that we can create ourselves by projecting freedom from a background of nothingness.

I must in brief compass connect the implications of this middle ground position with what I said previously about the two sides of self-realization. Accepting the element of destiny—the self I did not create but which is nevertheless the self I have to contend with—I can then seek to discover what my actual capabilities and talents are and for what sort of vocation—the "higher" self—I am most suited. The pursuit of this goal embraces both my own potentialities and the good I can contribute to the communities to which I belong. The point to be stressed here is that, considering that each of us is unique as an individual, each of us will have some contribution to make that no one else can make in the same way, so that if we fail in our task each of us will leave our communities poorer than they would otherwise have been. Our obligation points in two directions: one is the obligation to myself as a moral being to actualize my freedom responsibly, and the other is the obligation to my community not to deprive it of what I alone can contribute. I join hands with Roth when he suggests, in connection with my claim that the "unconditional validity of standards" is implied in all critical judgments (p. 28), that one may choose not to obey a particular obligation, but "cannot choose *not* to be obligated."

I turn now to the third issue to be considered: How is it possible for love to be commanded "when it means the free and whole-hearted giving of one person to another?" I recognize this difficult problem as the counterpart of the one I raised earlier about how to reconcile Royce's Absolute with individual freedom and crea-tivity. It seems to me legitimate to ask, in view of the Great Commandment, whether love is the sort of human response that can be subject to command. This question is prompted by our sense that whatever we are commanded to do must be a matter that is within our command or that we have command over and that thought leads us to ask whether love can be summoned on command. As an affection, love is an inclination of the whole person to another person and finds expression in a sincere concern for the welfare of the other. Love involves an understanding of the person to whom it is directed, and I believe that we are aware of the difference between having an affection for the other and having opinions or beliefs about that person. We have the sense that forming opinions is a process over which we have some con-trol, whereas we have no corresponding sense of having control over our affections or of being able to summon them at will. Hence it would seem that unless there is some other way to under-stand what being commanded means, we must conclude that love cannot be commanded. That conclusion cannot be final, however, because we are still left with the cornerstone of Christian teaching which is the commandment to love God and our neighbor.

The impasse we have reached should not surprise us since it points to a problem that Christianity has had to face from its very beginnings, the problem, namely, of overcoming the tension between law and love. This problem made itself felt in the Hebraic tradition as we learn from the Book of Jeremiah where the prophet, despairing over the failure of the people to keep the Commandments written on tables of stone, looks for a law that will be written "on their inward parts." For Christianity the prob-lem is deepened by the need to understand how love transcends law without annulling it and how there can be a law of love.

Without pretending to take on this complex theological issue,

I shall put forward some suggestions that may lead us to some understanding. A command must be understood, in part at least, as an imperative issued by a law-giver. For the Hebraic tradition God is cast in that role as the author of the Mosaic Law, a law Christianity acknowledges as part of its faith. I can understand how we can be commanded to follow the precepts of the Decalogue, both positive and negative, and of the second part of the Great Commandment enjoining us to love our neighbors as ourselves. The key is to understand the Christian *Agape*, not as a matter of "liking" the neighbor and self, but in the sense of care, concern, and regard for the well-being of the other and, further, not from our limited, self-interested, individual perspective but as far as possible from the view God takes of the other as a member of the divine Kingdom. It is this other-regarding standpoint which distinguishes *Agape* from both *Eros* and *Philia*, even if the latter two are not excluded from the relationship. What, however, are we to say of the commandment to love God?

The answer I am proposing is hinted at in the following sentence from Roth's essay: "Perhaps," he writes, "the injunction [to love God] signifies that we are obliged at least to examine the reasons why God is worthy of our love, and once these are recognized love will follow" as a consequence of our apprehending the intrinsic worthiness of God (p. 27). Suppose that for the moment we not think of "command" in the law-giver sense, but in another sense that is clearly enshrined in our language, according to which the intrinsic nature and virtue of a person is said to "command" our respect, affection, and devotion. The respect and affection, that is to say, are *elicited* from us by our apprehension of the *being* of the person. I believe this sense of "command" is well known and represents the sort of affection we experience, or is drawn from us, when we apprehend the virtue and the excellence of, for example, a person of steadfast loyalty under adverse circumstances, a person who sacrifices a great treasure for another, including perhaps life itself. In such cases we say that the person "commands" our respect, and to withhold it suggests that we have not properly apprehended the virtue standing before us. Perhaps in this way we can come to see how love of God can be commanded in the sense of being elicited from us by our apprehension of the intrinsic excellence of the Divine. This seems to me another way of saying what Roth means when he says that once the reasons why God is worthy of our love are recognized, "love will follow."

Perhaps some readers will perceive the hand of Jonathan Edwards in the foregoing; I freely acknowledge the fact. I do not know that any thinker has so successfully brought together in a unity of experience the *understanding* and the *affections*, which was the word he used for the biblical fruits of the Spirit—love, joy, faith, hope, humility, zeal etc. For Edwards, affections are *active* expressions of the inclination of one's heart when one apprehends the true nature and excellence of God, the Scriptures, the Church, the beauty of nature, and all that went by the name of the "things of religion." The central point of Edwards's conception—I regard it as his original contribution—is that affections follow upon or are "raised" by a *correct apprehension* of the intrinsic nature and excellence (worth) of the reality to which we are responding. He called this apprehension a "spiritual" understanding to distinguish it from a "purely notional" understanding that is devoid of a *sense* or a direct experience of what the words mean. For Edwards as for Locke, only those who have tasted the honey know what it means that honey is sweet. Thus the affection of love of God follows upon our having a sensible apprehension of the majesty, the goodness, the suffering love, and the beauty of the divine nature. The implication is that if a person does not have the appropriate affection, it is because the proper understanding is lacking. When, however, the spiritual understanding is there, the affection follows as a result. God's Gloria "commands" our love.

NOTES

1. I think here of Whitehead's comparison of arithmetic and religion; you *use* arithmetic, but you *are* religious.

2. We should note that Dewey used the term "intelligence" for a most basic virtue that embraced both knowledge and moral insight or wisdom and it certainly meant far more than "information."

Enlarging the Scope of Reason: Response to Vincent Colapietro

I AM GRATEFUL TO Colapietro for having brought together from various sources what I have had to say over the years about the recovery and reconstruction of experience and the closely related matter of enlarging the scope of reason. I often find that he is expressing what I want to say more adequately than I have been able to do myself, and I particularly appreciate his ability to combine sympathetic comprehension with constructive criticism. Since I find his expositions accurate and well pointed, I shall focus on his questions calling for further clarification. Although a number of issues are raised, the main emphasis is on the reconstruction of reason and especially my idea of living reason. Before commenting on his outline of the historical context for this reconstruction, I wish to indicate the three focal points that are involved. These are enlarging the scope of reason, recovering reason as a living force in individual life, and bringing importance or value once again within the compass of rational discourse.

Reason has been a watchword throughout the history of Western philosophy, but not enough attention has been paid to the fact that reason was not always understood in the same way during that time.[1] Augustine, for instance, echoing the Neoplatonic tradition, understood reason as the presence of order, measure, and form throughout the cosmos, and he could even cite music as one of its manifestations. By contrast, in Hume's thought that idea had vanished, and reason was reduced to the human power of reasoning deprived of its cosmic reach. If Hume's view is taken to be the whole truth, as it has been by many philosophers since his time, the truth in the Augustinian conception is lost. More important, however, than changes in the way reason was understood was the distinction between two particular functions of reason which goes back to Plato and Aristotle. Both acknowledged, on the one side, an analytic function aimed at distinguishing, describing, and expressing the nature of things in clear concepts, and, on the other, a synoptic or synthetic function meant to unite the items made distinct through analysis by disclosing the larger web of relations in which they stand, and to offer a unified picture of the world. These two functions were recognized by the medieval thinkers under the names of *ratio* and *intellectus*, and in modern philosophy by Kant's distinction between understanding (*Verstand*) and reason (*Vernunft*), the former as the analytic instrument of science and the latter as the means of achieving the unifying vision of philosophy. The emphasis in the philosophical thinking of the past half-century has been overwhelmingly on the side of the analytic function—witness the preference for piecemeal thinking over systematic and the continuing suspicion of metaphysics—so that reason in the synoptic sense has been forced into the background, if not denied altogether. As Colapietro rightly says, my concern for enlarging the scope of reason coincides with a recovery of the synoptic function and overcoming the unfortunate consequences of the narrow view such as the exclusion of value and importance from reason's arena.

The second aspect of reconstruction is the recovery of reason as a living power interpreting a person's experience and determining belief. Reason has its formal side, what Peirce called *logica docens*, in systems of logic and in the rational patterns of empirical inquiry; each is essential to reason, and I have no intention of denying its importance. To confine reason to its formal side, however, leaves out of account its active role in individual experience. It is that role I propose to call "living reason." If the name is new, the idea behind it reaches back to the dialectic of Plato, especially as we see it at work in the Socratic dialogues. There the discussion, whether about piety, justice, courage, or even the nature of virtue itself, is meant to engage the individual and to serve as a goad to self-knowledge so that a person comes to know what he or she believes and whether there are reasons for it. If Socrates's aim has not always been fulfilled, thwarted either by indifference or by the stubbornness born of the certainty that one already has the truth, his dialectic still remains as the best means for gaining self-understanding. Even Euthyphro, who leaves the discussion with a sarcastic remark about Socrates's making the words walk away, is not as certain as he was at the beginning of the dialogue that prosecuting his father for the death of the slave is an act of piety to the gods. Every Socratic discussion is an example of what I mean by living reason—an immanent interpretation and critique of individual experience. The authority exercised by reason stems from understanding and internalizing an intelligent course of thinking whereby the person is led to "see" some truth. Here the power of self-discovery is dependent not on the authority of another, but on a compelling insight stemming from one's own experience.

Another facet of living reason was suggested to me by Peirce's distinction between experiencing an argument—actually following or tracing out a rational sequence—and experiencing items denoted in an argument. The former is part of that internal dialogue, the sequence of interpreting signs, which is the substance of intelligent life. The subject may be any one you please, from mathematics to religion. The essential feature is the experience of reasonableness inherent in what we have encountered in the world, and it bears its own authority because we understand the rationality of the outcome in terms of the process through which it was reached. If it sounds strange to speak of experiencing a train of thought, that is only because we are so accustomed to thinking of experience as synonymous with what comes to us through the organs of sensation.

It was through the application of the idea of living reason that I sought to reinterpret the classical arguments for God in *Experience and God*. I shall not attempt to repeat that discussion; the main point is that, in my view, those arguments have no convincing power unless the individual understands the meaning of God involved by participating through the Bible and the Christian communities in the experience underlying the two relevant conceptions. In the ontological way God is apprehended as the Absolutely Exalted and in the cosmological way as the Necessarily Existent. It is not a matter of looking at a formal proof as a spectator from the outside, but rather of tracing a rational pattern immanent in one's own experience—in Peirce's terms, of experiencing the argument. At this point I shall only mention the third aspect of reconstruction—bringing value and importance back into the rational arena—because it is discussed below.

I find Colapietro's outline of the historical context for the reconstruction of reason very illuminating, especially since it embraces the "professional context" and the "broader intellectual milieu" (pp. 34ff.), both of which are important because they are challenges to which I was responding. I think the three reasons he gives for presenting the sketch are sound and bring out some important points—for instance, that connecting reason and subjectivity does not turn reason into something hopelessly "subjective" any more than accepting the fact that all thinking takes place within an historical order condemns reason to a hopeless relativism. On the contrary, attention to the role played by historical conditions in any type of interpretation not only points the relevance of thought to its own time, but also saves us from the illusion of having a rational insight that occurs nowhere and no when.

Much has been written about the relation of philosophy to its history since the time of Hegel and largely because he thought them so intimately connected. As has happened so often, the issue was soon polarized; on one side the historical factor was exaggerated and the result was historicism, while on the other side the bias against the need for an historical understanding led to the belief that we can penetrate to *die Sache selbst* with no concern for what others have thought about it. The latter approach has been called "philosophy without footnotes." It seems clear to me that both positions are untenable. Much is to be learned from seeing philosophical development as an historical dialectic between positions; the interaction reveals weaknesses and strengths and allows us to assess their explanatory power through comparisons. To deny the importance of this dialectic has been characteristic of most analytic philosophers in this century. These philosophers believe that the history of philosophy is not something to be engaged in; it is, however, curious that they have no objection to the discussion of previous philosophers if they happen to be Russell, Frege, or Wittgenstein!

Colapietro admirably sets forth (pp. 37ff.) what I take the role of Hegel's thought to be for understanding the present situation in philosophy—the need for reconstructing the idea of reason, the problems posed by exclusive emphasis on epistemology, and the status of what I call the "ontological principle." A great deal is to be learned from Hegel once we get over the idea that it is necessary to swallow Hegel or, even worse, to become an "Hegelian." No one has to accept his over-ambitious scheme of categories or his exaggerated rationalism which virtually eliminates evil and error to benefit from his many important insights. Among these I count his exposure of the abstract reason of the Enlightenment, his defense of empiricism and his criticism of its limitations, and his demonstration that pietism and rationalism, though diametrically opposed, meet in their common denial that there can be rational knowledge of God. The importance of Hegel in helping us to understand a philosophical development that has not yet run its course harbors a basic ambiguity. On one side, as Colapietro rightly emphasizes, Hegel saw the limitations of Kant's Understanding and sought to recover the rights of reason in substantive and not only regulative terms. On the other side, Hegel went too far, claimed too much for reason, and, in his claim that the real is the rational, declared that what is is what ought to be. The result was a backlash so intense that Kierkegaard, Hegel's most incisive critic, set out to find something that thought cannot think! I believe Hegel was right in recovering the broader conception of reason that had been attacked in the eighteenth century when the new science became the measure for all thought, and philosophy, at least in the sense of metaphysics, fell under a siege that has not yet been entirely lifted.[2] I believe that Hegel's critics were also right especially in their protest in the name of existence and the existing individual for whom the theoretical standpoint is but one among others and is transcended by personal engagement, commitment, and action.

The insights of what later became the philosophy of existence (I try to avoid "existentialism" because those it was supposed to designate invariably repudiated it) are genuine and stem from a personal concern for destiny and self-fulfillment in freedom for which there is not much room in Hegel's panlogism. If Hegel went too far in his rationalism, his critics made the same mistake but in the opposite direction by absolutizing those features of life and world which Hegel subordinated. Colapietro captures the point very nicely (p. 37) when he says that "rupture," "difference," "fragmentation" are the watchwords of postmodern culture and on that very account mediation, integration, and reconciliation are "likely to be met with the deepest suspicion."

Are the evils of Hegel's totalizing reason to be overcome by totalizing nihilism, the reversal of values, the absurd and the contra-
dictory? It is a great irony that the aftermath of Hegel should itself
bear witness to one of his basic ideas; what other philosophy
succeeded so completely in bringing about its own opposite?

Colapietro is correct in detecting two other points where I find
Hegel's insights of importance (pp. 41, 42ff.)—one concerns his
judgment about the skepticism of modern philosophy concerning
the relation between thought and things, and the other is his critique of Kant's critical philosophy and its influence on what
Dewey called the "epistemology industry."

Every student of Western philosophy knows that from the time
of Plato and Aristotle there was a natural belief in an immanent
rationality or *logos* in the world and a coordination between this
structure and the *logos* inherent in human reason. This belief was
expressed in Aristotle's parallelism between *Ta legomena*—what
can be rationally said of things—and *Ta onta*—the real things
themselves. Whatever we can know through experience and reflection is knowledge or truth about these real things. This natural
belief persisted at least until the end of the seventeenth century
where it received a new formulation in Spinoza's "The order and
connection of ideas is the same as the order and connection of
things." It is this belief which I call the "ontological principle."
This principle had never been more than a natural assumption and
was rarely stated; it remained part of an unwritten philosophy.
Nothing, however, is more likely to bring an assumption to light
than its being brought into question, as indeed it was chiefly by
the skeptical empiricism of Hume, but also by Kant's criticism.

Hegel understood this problem very well; referring to the coordination between thought and things, he wrote:

> In modern times a doubt has for the first time been raised on this
> point in connection with the difference alleged to exist between
> the products of our thoughts and the things in their own nature.
> This real nature of things, it is said, is very different from what
> we make out of them. The divorce between thought and thing is
> mainly the work of the critical philosophy, and runs counter to
> the conviction of all previous ages, that their agreement was a
> matter of course. *The antithesis between them is the hinge on which
> modern philosophy turns.*[3]

Hegel could have reinforced his point by citing the phenomenalism of Hume and later British empiricism according to which we do not know things in the "external world" but only our own ideas. Commenting further on the "hinge" just noted, Hegel continued:

> Meanwhile the natural belief of men gives the lie to it. In common life we reflect, without particularly reminding ourselves that this is the process of arriving at the truth, and we think without hesitation, and in the firm belief that thought coincides with thing. . . . It marks the diseased state of the age when we see it adopt the despairing creed that our knowledge is only subjective.[4]

We are in a better position than Hegel to see how the matter worked out. Those who refused to accept the natural belief had only two alternatives: either to embrace subjectivism as the truth, or to attempt to recover the ancient principle through some form of argument. Kant's transcendental deduction—intended to guarantee an objective synthesis as over against the subjective one—may be taken as an instance of the second alternative. I cannot take the matter further here, but I believe that neither of these approaches can succeed given the terms of the problem. The point I do want to emphasize, however, is that the quest for objectivity which followed the rejection of the natural belief in the coincidence of thought and thing established epistemology at the center of philosophy and postponed the discussion of first-order questions.

Hegel's thought is also important for its treatment of another problem stemming from the overemphasis on the theory of knowledge; we may call it the paradox at the heart of critical philosophy. He agreed that testing the capabilities and limitations of an instrument is a needed task. But what, he asked, if the instrument to be tested is thought itself? The adequacy of external tools can be determined because we can analyze them and compare one specimen with another. But is our thought a "tool" in this sense, and does it make no difference when the object of criticism is the same as the faculty carrying out the criticism? Hegel's answer was succinct and to the point. He accepted the need for criticism even of thought itself, but he could not accept the Kantian form, which he described as "knowing before you know."

Hegel, that is, did not believe that there can be an introduction to philosophical thinking—a *prolegomenon*—which is supposed to determine *before* the actual discussion of questions about God, freedom, etc. whether our powers are adequate for the task. Hegel's idea of criticism was of a different sort. Kant, he thought, viewed the activity of understanding and reason abstractly in terms of their formal features—universality and necessity—and *antecedent* to their employment in thinking actual subject matter. Hegel's idea was that the capacity of our categories cannot be estimated when they are merely idling in our understanding, but only when they are at work in analyzing the entire range of experience of which the activity of the mind is only a part. For Hegel, criticism means the categories criticizing themselves, for when they are at work in the process of inquiry we have an opportunity to determine when they are illuminating and make coherent sense of the world and when they fail by distorting or impoverishing experience because of their abstractness of other limitations. Thus, Hegel's approach insists that we proceed to the philosophical task itself and judge the results in terms of what a particular idea, category, theory can *do* and whether it renders experience more transparent and significant or more opaque and problematic. The day of judgment is concerned with the outcome of thought at work, in contrast to the Kantian way which insists that we postpone inquiry until we know whether or not our thought is capable of succeeding. It was the prior critique that Hegel branded as "knowing before you know" and compared it to the youth who wanted to learn how to swim without going into the water. Hegel saw the futility of philosophical preliminaries and, like the philosopher of experience he was, decided that philosophers should emulate the scientists (i.e., systematic inquirers in any field and not just natural sciences) who, with no thought for the question "How is knowledge possible?" just "go ahead and know." In this way attention is shifted from *foundations* to *outcomes*; philosophical positions can be judged only in a dialectical way where we can determine the relative merits and weaknesses of a set of ideas by comparing what these ideas can do in the way of making sense out of experience. It is a tribute to the classical American philosophers that they learned this lesson, avoided the seductions of epistemology, and offered instead constructive philosophies far more significant and enduring than any of Russell's annual attempts to transcend sense data and reach the "external world."

Colapietro expresses in a most perceptive way (pp. 00ff.) the development of patterns of intelligibility and the need for reflective thinking to detect and state explicitly the pattern dominant in a given period. The task, in the nature of the case, is difficult since thinking *with* a set of ideas defining a unified outlook cannot be accompanied by a thinking *about* the adequacy of these same ideas. As Colapietro rightly sees, my appeal to a "dialectical arena" in which philosophical positions become related through critical comparison is meant to be the proving ground for making clear the validity of any position. The rationalists of the seventeenth century, for example, riding on the high tide of a universal reason, could not see for themselves the extent of their neglect of experience or their reduction of the perceptual world to a set of confused concepts. The empiricists, in turn, while adept at exposing the abstractness of the previous systems of reason, were unaware of the narrow conception of experience developed at their hands. The limitations of any standpoint cannot be discovered solely from the inside; a wider perspective is needed which forces a position beyond itself. This idea was used to great effect by Hegel when he insisted that a philosophy must be able to show its applicability not merely to some selected portion of experience but to experience in its widest scope. An atomism, for example, can be expected to be quite successful in accounting for parts, for what is disparate, and what is relatively independent of the wholes to which it is related, but how can such a position do justice to the phenomena of organism and internal relatedness? The answer is that it cannot.

The idea of a critical comparison between philosophical positions will be met with the question "What are the criteria for judgment?" This question, moreover, is often accompanied by the assumption that each position will insist on its own and the situation will be hopeless. This is a counsel of despair and is out of touch with what actually happens. All philosophies seek (or should) to articulate and interpret the widest possible range of experience; hence, it is fair to say that all must be judged in terms of internal coherence, coherence as between the various dimensions of experience—morality, science, art—and the extent to which the position illuminates experience and enhances its quality. At an even more general level, there are two guiding principles to be respected; the first is that the world as described and interpreted must not be poorer than the world directly encountered and enshrined in cumulative experience and common sense. This principle speaks against reductionism in the "nothing but" sense; it does not, however, preclude the analyses and explanations which are necessary for knowledge, but which also transform the things of primary experience. Hegel put this point very well; in knowing nature, he wrote, we want to exhibit nature as she *is*, but in order to do so, we must show her as she is *not*, that is, as shorn of her warmth and color, a victim of gravity, energy, and atoms. The resolution of this paradox, for which we are indebted to Whitehead and Dewey, is not to deny the well-founded abstractions necessary for knowledge, but to understand their proper status and not allow them to *replace* the concrete things they are meant to explain.

The second guiding principle is that a philosophy should make the world more intelligible than it was before and not nullify the testimony of pervasive experience. Berkeley had something of this in mind when he claimed to "side in all things with the mob" and criticized philosophers for raising dust and then complaining that they cannot see. As an example, consider McTaggart's ingenious arguments to show that time is unreal and the jolt they gave to familiar expectations about "yesterday" and "tomorrow." C. D. Broad, in his exhaustive commentary on *The Nature of Existence*, found himself baffled by McTaggart's discussion about time and ended by saying that it contained arguments no one could refute in support of a conclusion that no one could accept! The moral is that dialectical skill must not outrun reality.

I referred before to some questionable assumptions often made about criteria and their use in evaluation. Colapietro calls attention to what I believe is the most important point that needs to be made in this connection. He writes:

> . . . the various criteria by which the rival schemes are evaluated are not completely fixed in advance of the actual work of comparative evaluation, however secure a criterion (for example, clarity) or set of criteria might be at the outset. The criteria themselves are likely to evolve in the course of the comparison [p. 47].

Peirce did much to discredit the idea, well represented by Descartes but also to be found in Aristotle, that criteria or first principles are "prior" to the thought they determine and are absolutely fixed and certain. Peirce reinterpreted the classical "laws of logic" and claimed that their validity becomes apparent when they are understood in themselves and seen to be the preconditions of all inquiry. In actual practice a relation of mutual support between these preconditions and the results of inquiry becomes evident. Inquiry controlled by the logical principles is seen to lead to conclusions that command the consensus of the scientific community and this consensus in turn bears witness to the validity of the principles themselves.

I believe there is an even more perspicuous example of the point Colapietro is making, and it is furnished by Descartes. Consider the famous criteria of clear and distinct, the marks of intuitive certainty. In carrying out his program of doubt, Descartes tells us that when he came upon the *cogito* he had reached what could not be doubted and hence had to be certain. It is not always noted that his next move was to ask himself what there was about the "I think, therefore I am" which formed the basis of his certainty. That is, *subsequent* to his having the specimen of certainty in hand, he decided that it was the clarity and distinctness of his apprehension which was the guarantee of certainty. It is not that he *first* had these criteria before him and identified the *cogito* by applying them; it was, rather, the other way around. The criteria were already ingredient in the specimen and were subsequently abstracted. If the application of criteria, in our case for the comparison of different philosophical positions, were seen in this dialectical sense, there would be less need to insist that there be total agreement and certainty about criteria *in advance*, and more willingness to get on with actual comparisons which in any case can only be postponed by multiplying preliminary discussions about criteria before they are set to work.

Colapietro's discussion "Enlarging the Scope of Reason" (pp. 51ff.) is admirable in that it highlights the four points which I think are important to be stressed here. They are the nature and criticism of abstractions, precision in thought and the need to determine the degree of precision needed in a given case by appeal to the purpose of the analysis, the connection between enlarging reason and broadening experience, and the integration of our many purposes by appeal to what is *important*, something that leads on to the concern that *importance* (and value in general) not be excluded from the scope of reason. I agree with Colapietro's criticism (pp. 53–56) that much more needs to be said about integration and importance than I have thus far provided. I cannot hope to make up so large a deficiency here, but I can offer some pointers on both heads. As regards importance, the main point to be stressed is that value, significance, relevance are ingredient in all experience in the form of selective attention in which judgments (if this term seems too strong, we may say "perceptions," but these are also judgments) of what "counts" or has value for some purpose are expressed. Both James and Whitehead emphasized this fact about experience and argued that it is forced out of the picture by the belief that there is such a thing as "mere fact" devoid of the connections in which importance and relevance are found. Whitehead's account is especially compelling because of his insistence that both "importance" and "matter of fact" are required because we concentrate by reason of a sense of importance, and when we do so we attend to matter of fact. But recognizing the bias in favor of fact engendered mainly by the sciences, Whitehead added one of his characteristically arch comments: "Those people," he wrote, "who in a hard headed way confine their attention to matter of fact do so by reason of their own sense of the importance of such an attitude."[5] We might further express the mutual connection between the two by adding that the sense of importance is itself matter of fact. In this, as in other philosophical matters, I would stress the importance of purpose and of having as clear an idea as possible about what we are trying to achieve. Importance figures at two points in all purposive thought and action; there is the importance to be assigned to the end in view, and there is the determination of what is important for the achievement of that end. While I do not believe there is or can be any *formula* for the integration of our many purposes or the harmonization of conflicting aims, some guidelines are possible and these stem from what I believe is and should be the matter of ultimate importance for all: namely, the concern for defining the substance of self-realization or a fruitful and significant life for all human beings and for seeking to bring about the reality of all the communities through which alone that realization is possible.

The two guidelines that follow are to be seen as ordering principles to serve the purpose of harmonizing different and sometimes conflicting interests and aims. The first is directed to the individual and concerns the choice that every person must face in finding an overarching purpose which expresses the self that he or she means to become. Such a purpose coincides with a vocation fulfilling the person as a whole and at the same time providing a measure for bringing about a harmony of the interests and lesser purposes which abound in every human life. Finding our fundamental vocation, as I noted earlier in response to Roth's questions, is not an easy task and requires a knowledge of ourselves and of our talents and capabilities, together with a sense of what we as individuals are best fitted to contribute to the common good of the immediate communities in which we live and ultimately to the community of mankind. The second principle concerns the causes to which our communities are devoted and the importance of efforts to realize a vision of a worthwhile life for all mankind in a viable world that includes both the physical environment and a just social order. The magnitude of this task is obviously enormous because of the formidable obstacles that stand in the way when we seek to extend and sustain the cooperative and life-enhancing power of a community with loyal members. Chief among these obstacles are the force of individual selfishness and the drive to compete in the hope of attaining a power that is rarely used for the common good. The optimism usually associated with democracy and secularization have contributed greatly to loss of any strong sense of the reality of evil both in ourselves and in our institutions. There is that lower self we like to hide or, even worse, refuse to admit that it exists at all. Augustine expressed our capacity for self-deception in a classic passage; he confessed that he like to think that he was more himself in those things in himself of which he approved than in those things of which he disapproved. James was right when he claimed that the Judeo-Christian tradition and the Buddhist tradition are more profound and realistic in outlook in virtue of their recognition of the power of evil in all its forms.

Colapietro in his summary statement about enlarging the scope of reason admirably sums up the characteristics which an expanded reason would enjoy. It would be *dialectical* in taking account of alternative perspectives and in seeking to correct one-sidedness of any sort; it would *historical* in allowing for the role played by the culture of a given era in shaping the reflective thought of the time; it would be *fallibilistic* in rejecting claims to certainty and in remaining open to revision; it would be *contextual* in recognizing the different purposes expressed in the different dimensions of experience—scientific, ethical, aesthetic, etc.—while seeking to relate them to each other; it would be *interpretive* in insisting on the discursive character of all thought and in resisting appeals to intuitive apprehension transcending the use of signs; it would be *participatory* in involving the engagement of the total personality in thinking and in overcoming the spectator stance in relation to experience; it would be *conciliatory* in the cause of advancing our understanding and not over-zealous in polemical intent. If I understand him correctly, Colapietro believes as I do that if our conception of reason were expanded along these lines, we could avoid, on the one hand, the totalizing of reason exhibited by Hegel, and the narrowing of reason to a merely analytic function on the other.

Notes

1. For example, in the discussions about reason and faith of some years ago prompted by Karl Barth's attack on natural theology, it was invariably assumed that faith was the problematic concept standing in need of extensive clarification, while the nature of reason was supposed to be clear and obvious.

2. Kant, it will be recalled, distinguished the *critical* stance from the *dogmatic*, the former being the transcendental approach or the tribunal that does not take a side in a metaphysical dispute, while the latter takes a definite position about an issue in question. I believe Hegel was correct when he claimed that Kant, in making the Understanding the measure of *all* knowledge, ceased being critical and became dogmatic. The issue is whether the aim and method of the special sciences are proper criteria for judging philosophical interpretation.

3. *Encyclopaedia*, section 22; emphasis added.

4. Ibid.

5. *Modes of Thought* (New York: Macmillan, 1938), p. 5.

Metaphysics, Experience, Being, and God: Response to Robert C. Neville

IF I UNDERSTAND HIM CORRECTLY, the idea underlying Neville's interpretation of my thinking about philosophical and religious issues is that, while I have no identifiable metaphysical system, I do have a metaphysical position (p. 79), so that out of my extensive discussion of the nature of experience there emerges a conception of being and of God. I have the distinct impression that he regards the position in question as in need of a more explicit formulation than I have given it and, hence, that much of his discussion is meant to help overcome the deficiency. I believe that Neville's underlying idea is correct, but I think we need to be clear about the meaning of "system." The word "sustema" in Greek meant the bringing of many statements together in order to overcome contradiction and thus achieve coherence and comprehensiveness in the treatment of any subject. In this sense it seems to me that we need such an approach, but that it would be better to speak, as Neville does of his own thinking, about being "systematic" as opposed to what was called some decades ago "piecemeal" philosophy which was aimed at the consideration of minute points. It is difficult, however, especially after Hegel, to avoid the association of system with a comprehensive and all-embracing philosophical edifice that is complete and thus closed. As I indicated in response to Colapietro, I do not believe in system in this sense, but that need not mean that our thinking should not be systematic.

Neville is right in calling attention to the two traditions that have determined most of my thought—the developmemt of American philosophy starting with Edwards and moving to the pragmatists, and the tradition of German idealism which for me meant largely the tension between Kant and Hegel—and I can see more clearly now than ever before why Neville should also be right in saying (p. 71) that metaphysical considerations are much more prominent in my dealing with the German tradition than with the American. The difference at this point was due largely to the fact that metaphysics is prominent in the thought of the German idealists (and Royce), so much of which was focused for me by Paul Tillich and his metaphysical theology, and, apart from Royce, I had not yet encountered the metaphysical underpinnings of the pragmatists. I have on other occasions made Neville's point (p. 71) about the strictures imposed by my academic situation; in my early days at Yale the need for teaching Kant and Hegel was paramount, and I was less than autonomous in choosing areas for research. At that time, despite the existence of an American Studies program, there was not much attention being paid to the American philosophers (Charles Hendel was an exception because of his interest in Dewey), and I could not move in that direction until much later. Although I had worked on Royce's idea of community and his philosophy of religion, I was not able to follow up on that in either teaching or research because interest in Royce was at a low ebb (in 1950 virtually all his works were out of print), and what interest there was in the American thinkers was focused on Dewey, James, and Peirce whose thought was just being discovered.

Before turning to Neville's comments on my autobiographical essay of 1980, "Experience and the Boundary Between Philosophy and Religion" (p. 72), I want to mention an occurrence that was of the greatest importance in turning my attention to the basic ideas of the pragmatists. I was familiar earlier on with Peirce's ideas about signs, interpretation, and community through study of those writings which Royce cited in *The Problem of Christianity*, but I had not read extensively in either James or Dewey (except for James's *Varieties* and Dewey's *A Common Faith*). I no longer recall exactly when, but Ernest Hocking with whom I had been corresponding about Royce sent me an article which he had written about Dewey. It began with Hocking's confession that he began to learn from Dewey only when he stopped reading him for the purpose of showing that he was all wrong. I had no difficulty in seeing that I had been doing the same thing and that I really did not know Dewey's thought in any depth, but, rather, was reacting to Sidney Hook's picture of Dewey. According to Hook, the importance of Dewey was in his central emphasis on science, his critical attitude toward religion, and his suspicion of much traditional philosophy. At that juncture I decided to find out about Dewey for myself and I soon discovered two fundamental ideas that I would build on in the years to come. One was his reconstruction of the conception of experience following on his critique of the view of experience associated with Locke and Hume. The other was his attack on the enterprise of epistemology which he thought was engaged with issues such as how to reach the "external world," issues posed by the erroneous idea that our knowledge is not about real things but about only our immediate sense impressions.

To return to the autobiographical essay: I am pleased that Neville makes the "non-postmodern assumption" that my own account of how ideas developed for me "has some standing," but I shall not join that issue here, despite my belief that the contrary assumption is absurd. He rightly focuses on two points (p. 72): first, that for quite some time I believed one could accept the Kantian theory of human thought and its negative consequences for metaphysics, while preserving the metaphysical questions for treatment in some other way; and, second, that after reading Hegel and the American philosophers, I decided that the foregoing belief was wrong and that a more critical stance toward the critical philosophy itself was in order, along with a plumbing of the resources provided by the reconstructed idea of experience for dealing with metaphysical questions. I agree entirely with Neville's point that, in my view, experience has its own logos within it and has an objective reach of which it was deprived by the British empiricists. Both features qualify experience as a reliable medium of disclosure which I expressed through the idea that the subjectivist's formula, "the world takes place in experience," is to be replaced by a realist formula, "experience takes place in the world."

Neville's next point is quite crucial and calls for considerable explanation on my part. Actually, his point is two points, but they are closely connected. First, he says correctly that for me experience is not essentially an epistemological category but an alternative to the Aristotelian category of causality as the primary access to what there is.

His second point is that for me experience has a more direct metaphysical bearing, by which he means my proposal that experience might serve as what I call a "firmament" for theology in much the same way as Being had performed this function for so many centuries. This point must command our attention since it determines the main purpose of Neville's essay: namely, to construe my theory of experience as a metaphysics. The previous point, however, is not without its own importance in this connection, since, as I argued in *The Analogy of Experience*, experience has a distinctive status in the scheme of things as an emergent when seen from an evolutionary standpoint. We can conceive of a time in which the capacity to read signs—Peirce's "thirdness"—did not yet exist and the relations between things were all dyadic so that nothing of the nature of experience was possible. So understood, experience ceases to be a merely epistemological element and assumes a proper status in the structure of the universe.

In addressing Neville's adventurous proposal to read my conception of experience as a metaphysics, I think it best to look upon it as a thought experiment since, as he says, the procedure "does some violence" to my position and had I wanted to express it that way I would have. Hence, in what follows I shall be considering his reading largely in terms of whether it is implicit in what I have written and whether I would now subscribe to it in its new form.

As I understand it, Neville's procedure is to reread my analyses of experience as leading to a speculative understanding of God and of Being, two classical metaphysical topics. I believe this procedure was suggested to him by my idea that experience could be made to serve as a "firmament" for theology in the way Being had served in the tradition of Christian theology. Neville begins by asking about the relation between experience and Being, postponing the question about the relation between experience and theology. There is no problem about the postponement since he discusses the matter in the succeeding pages; nevertheless, the relation between experience and theology is for me prior in importance, because it was in that connection that the idea of assigning to experience the role previously given to Being first occurred to me. Moreover, I developed this idea at great length in *The Analogy of Experience* where I explained it as a matter of principle under the name *analogia experientiae* and applied it in expressing the nature of God, of Christ, and of the Christian community. Neville does not mention this discussion here and therefore it is not clear to me whether he is taking it into account in his reading of my conception of experience as metaphysics. The reason for my concern is that to understand what I mean by assigning to experience the role previously assigned to Being it is necessary to take-in the context marked out by my reinterpreting of the ancient enterprise of "faith seeking understanding." The understanding sought for was carried out through philosophical concepts, the most important of which was Being. As Neville rightly notes (p. 73), I do not equate Being and experience, but I do have in mind the idea that the traditional *analogia entis* might be reworked as the analogy of experience, especially at a time when the classical notion of Being is no longer as familiar as it once was.

Perhaps the best way to proceed is for me to comment on the particular points Neville makes in carrying out his task as a basis for asking what further light is thrown on the picture by bringing in further considerations drawn from *The Analogy of Experience.*

The idea that for me Being is the "capability to enter into experience" is certainly consistent with what I have written over the years, even if I have not actually stated it this way. I would agree, moreover, that this view echoes the Platonic conception of Being as power as over against the approach of Aristotle for whom Being was understood in terms of how a thing has its properties, essentially or accidentally. I have on occasions explicitly identified Being with power in connection with a problem which cannot be dealt with here, but which I shall merely mention. The problem concerns how Being is to be given a definite character which it must have if it is to be intelligible at all, if every definite character *ipso facto* excludes something. Here power has always seemed to me the best candidate. Neville is correct in saying that for me experience is an interaction, a term I believe is better than "transaction" (Dewey abandoned the latter term because it seemed to play into the hand of those like Russell who called pragmatism the philosophy of American business, citing as well James's "cash value," "bank notes," and "success"). Not all of our experienced interactions are experiential in character, since, as Neville rightly says, there are mechanical interactions as well. The phenomena, for example, from which the geologist reconstructs the past history of continents, mountains, rivers, etc., are of the latter sort. Fortunately, the natural objects entering into the interactions leave characteristic signs on each other, and it is through knowing how to read these signs that the past is reconstructed.

The comparisons with Kant are helpful; I would agree with him that what cannot enter into experience cannot be known, but I would claim in addition that what cannot in principle enter into experience cannot be real. Neville is right in seeing that this claim rules out unexperienceable things-in-themselves as inconceivable, because on my view whatever can be conceived must be accessible to experience. I accept his statement that I take from Peirce the idea that experience is *subjunctive*—"a thing is capable of entering experience if it would enter experience under the appropriate experiential conditions." The "would" here must be carefully understood. In my view, the term indicates a genuine mode of Being coinciding with real possibility. This view runs counter to the belief that whatever modes of Being there may be are only logical in character and also to the nominalist doctrine that existence there and then is the only "real" mode. This view is expressed by Carnap in *Meaning and Necessity*, where the modal operator for existence is counted as "empirical" while those for possibility and necessity are merely "L-true." Kant must bear some responsibility here because of his treatment of the modal categories; these categories, he declared, have to do not with conceptual content, but with the relation of that content to the mind. What this means becomes clear when we come to his "schematization" of the categories and learn that what distinguishes possibility, necessity, and existence from each other is a temporal quantifier with existence as the recurrent mode. Thus, possibility is existence at some time or other, existence is existence at this time, and necessity is existence at all times. This understanding of modality leaves only existence as a real mode of Being and in this respect coincides with the linguistic nominalism that stems from Ockham.

So much for experience, for the time being at least; let me go on to Neville's account of what I mean by God, presumably as this is to be discovered by taking my theory of experience as a metaphysics. Neville's first paragraph (p. 75) focuses the discussion, and while I believe he is correct in the main, much more needs to be said if misunderstanding is to be avoided. He begins by reiterating my idea that experience might play the role in philosophical theology that being played for so long a time in the Western tradition. He explains this role as follows: "being was the concept according to which theologians both distinguished and related God and the world" (p. 75). This is true if it is understood that "world" includes the human self, so that the relation is not seen as a purely cosmological affair. He continues, "For Smith, the concept of experience functions so as to distinguish and connect God and the world" (p. 75). This is also the case, but Neville's next comment—"The analogy goes little further" (p. 75)—stands greatly in need of correction, and the reason has to do with what I mean by a "firmament" for theology, something not to be understood only in relation to the idea of being. Neville here takes being as the model, presumably because I said experience might function something like the way being did, and says, "Smith does not mean that God is pure experience as many theologians had claimed God is pure being." Here Neville is certainly right; being, though it could be and indeed was seen as a medium of *expression*, is not a medium in the same sense as I take experience to be. As I shall point out, however, the analogy of experience I am proposing does go further than Neville supposes, since it provides a theological basis for the expression of a faith with *understanding* and the particular experiences through which theological concepts are to be made intelligible. My impression is that this view itself will not be intelligible until I try to explain more fully what I meant by a "firmament" for theology and what particular problems the idea was supposed to resolve.

A continuing problem facing Christian theologians was posed by the fact that it is not possible to pass directly from the biblical writings to a conceptual and systematic formulation of Christian doctrine. A way of approach, a logic, and a number of basic concepts are needed, and, since every theology is written at a particular time, these essentials will stem from "secular" sources. Those who founded Christian theology looked to the systems of Greek philosophy for the required concepts and an underlying framework for thought which I call a "firmament." The key concept involved was that of being, and it was used, as Neville rightly

says, by theologians who differed from each other in their doctrines and even in their conception of being. The problem about
the firmament took on a new shape as a result of the Reformation
and, later on, the Enlightenment. The Reformers looked with
considerable suspicion on the philosophically oriented theologies
of the Middle Ages and demanded that theology be more closely
derived from the Bible. From the side of the philosophers of the
Enlightenment came severe attacks on the validity of metaphysics,
including a nominalist trend resulting in the replacement of the
concept of being with that of existence. In short, being and the
metaphysical traditions had fallen on evil days, and the question
was, "Is it possible to continue the development of theology in
the classical way, or must some new firmament be found?"

It is in relation to this question that I proposed experience as a
viable firmament aimed, on the one hand, at maintaining a philosophical approach to theology and, on the other, keeping it in
closer touch with the *religious* dimension of life. That the problem
of the firmament was no minor one (it still exists, but in subdued
tones) can be seen from even a brief survey of the various attempts
that were made to resolve it. Some religious thinkers accepted
the demise of metaphysics and adopted the new conception of
philosophy as essentially linguistic analysis and logic for the articulation of religious belief. This approach meant conceptual
analysis of religious utterances—what was known as "God talk"—
and was fideistic in the sense that no cognitive claims could be
made for these utterances. Other thinkers decided to abandon
philosophy as a firmament and sought to make history, sociology,
or literature serve the same purpose. At the other end of the
spectrum was the attempt by Karl Barth to eliminate any form
of mediation for theology, but especially philosophy, in the interest of developing purely biblical theology independent of all secular thought. This approach results in a kind of religious positivism
which has affinities with fundamentalism, except that in Barth's
case there is a mountain of sophistication and historical scholarship
that stands in stark contrast to the anti–intellectualism and even
obscurantism of most fundamentalists. Some thinkers following
the lead of Wittgenstein have reshaped theology so that competence with religious symbols, including doctrine, is understood
through his idea of learning a language game and is the channel

whereby the individual becomes engaged with religious realities. On this view, however, the idea of any correspondence between doctrine and these realities virtually falls from sight, and it may well be asked whether this is not too high a price to pay in order to show that religious and theological expressions are not "theoretical" descriptions and explanations of the sort found in science.

I fear that I have become too involved in a substantive way with an issue that I wished to use only for the purpose of showing what I mean by the firmament problem and why I proposed experience as a resolution. I hope it is clear that I wish to remain in the tradition of philosophical theology in which metaphysics plays a central role and that I do not believe that Barth's rejection of extra-biblical mediation is a real possibility or that the Wittgensteinian and other linguistic approaches are adequate.

With this clarification in mind, let us return to Neville's discussion of the idea of God. He makes central my statement that "the God who can appear to the religious consciousness as the first certainty becomes, for speculative philosophy, the ultimate problem." While I still believe that this statement expresses an important point, I am not sure that I would want to use it as the basis for a comprehensive position chiefly because it stands in need of clarification and expansion. "Certainty," as it now appears to me, is too strong; "conviction" or "article of faith" might be more appropriate since I always want to stress the element of risk involved in faith and certainty is too safe and complacent. The underlying idea remains, however, and Neville points to it when he says that I set myself "over against Hume's tradition of philosophy of religion, according to which God needs to be inferred out of experiential elements" (p. 75). Religious faith or conviction does not *start* with argumentation or dialectical attempts to guarantee the reality of God; instead, it stands on that faith as it is expressed in biblical terms— "in the beginning, God . . ." and "in the beginning was the Word. . . ." Whatever has been maintained by later theologians, biblical religion does not traffic in an inferred God, but finds itself rooted initially in direct experience. Even the Book of Job, which contains more dialectical treatment of a basic theological issue than any other in the Jewish Bible, has for its theme not *whether* God exists, but rather how we are to understand the nature and ways of God in the midst of bitter and perplexing experience.

The truth that the religious consciousness does not begin with dialectic, however, is itself only a beginning, a beginning that calls for an articulation of the faith from which it sets out. This articulation takes two forms, one directed inward and the other outward. The former represents the desire to *understand the meaning* of the initial faith, while the latter seeks to relate that understanding to other beliefs in the culture at large in the form of replying to questions posed by critics and skeptics. Here I am concerned with the inward articulation, but I shall pause to enter a word of explanation about the outward form which has often been called by the misleading name of "apologetics." The Greek term means "to answer questions" for the purpose of making a position more understandable and better known; there is no implication that one is "apologizing" for the position as if one were ashamed of espousing it.

Neville rightly points out that I put myself in the tradition reaching as far back as Augustine known as *fides quaerens intellectum* or "faith seeking understanding," which I called above the inward form of articulation. Here I would underline his point that within this approach there is plenty of room for inference, but it is always in the middle of experience and never at "stages of initial premisses." The task, then, is to seek to understand the experience of God at hand, but also the faith in and about God to be found in the biblical writings and theological interpretation which define the religious community into which one has been introduced.[1]

It is important that Neville stresses the distinction I make between so-called immediate experience and direct experience (p. 76). As he correctly says, "If we had any truly immediate experience, we would not know we had it," and the reason is clear: all thinking, judgment, apprehension of meaning takes place through the mediation of signs and is therefore discursive in nature. I do not, however, follow those who suppose that ruling out immediate experience as such must mean that experience is essentially an inferential affair. It is for this reason that I speak of *direct* experience, which means encountering whatever it is that we experience or being in its presence. When two persons are in conversation, for example, I claim that each experiences the other directly and that it is highly artificial to say that each *infers* the existence of the other. I do maintain in the religious context, however, that, if we take mysticism as a special case, all cases of divine encounter or disclosure are such that there is at the same time an encounter with *something else*. That is to say, that there is, as the entire Judeo-Christian tradition shows, always a disclosing medium—person, event, word—through which experience comes. Moses and the burning bush, Isaiah's vision of Holiness, Paul on the road to Damascus are cases in point.

Neville takes up the second part of my statement that God is the ultimate problem from the standpoint of speculative philosophy or metaphysics and asks how we are to understand metaphysically what is for experience a basic presupposition. The question is legitimate and relevant, but there is something important in my statement that is omitted. The context was the relation between religion and philosophy, and my point is that, while religion has God as a foundation, God is an ultimate problem for philosophy insofar as a philosopher asks the ultimate question of why there is anything at all, or, in Whitehead's language, asks for the ultimate fact without which there would be no facts at all. A philosopher may, of course, stop short of putting such a question and rest with the belief that it has no meaning or settle for the self-sufficiency of Nature so that an advance to the problem of God is not necessary.[2]

I think that Neville expresses very well what I seek to do in the analysis, not of "religious experience" as he clearly understands, but of the religious dimension of experience as defined through the distinction between the Holy and the profane and the idea that encounter with the Holy occasions *the* religious question about the ground and goal of human life.

Moreover, it is important to stress, as he does, that it is "not merely our causes and purposes, but the ground of the contingent world as such, the purpose of human life as such" (p. 77) that are in question. Neville's comparison with Tillich's position has a point, but it must be stated somewhat diffferently. He has Tillich claiming that because we exist and have an ultimate concern there must be a divine ground and purpose, whereas for me all this is a question—that is, perhaps life is experienced as non-contingent, nihilistic, or empty. The last point is correct, but Tillich is an

Augustinian and he would not invoke a "because" principle in moving from existence and concern to God. His article "The Two Types of the Philosophy of Religion" makes this clear; the cosmological type appeals to a causal argument (Aquinas), whereas the ontological type finds the divine present in the first principles of *Sapientia*—*Verum, Bonum, Esse*—(Augustine, Anselm). There is another difference involved: Tillich was speaking as a theologian from within what he called the "theological circle," while I am approaching from the side of the philosopher who cannot take the theological content for granted.

Neville's discussion ends with a question and a final point with a retrospective and a prospective side (pp. 79–80); I shall close my response with a brief consideration of each. "It is an interesting question," he writes, ". . . whether he believes that the setting forth of a large-scale metaphysical hypothesis would necessarily betray his deep empiricism." My direct answer to this question is, No, and indeed it could not be otherwise in view of the position about the human predicament, the nature of God, the significance of Christ, and the role of the religious community, all of which I developed in *The Analogy of Experience*. Whether Neville would regard this as a "large-scale metaphysical hypothesis," I cannot say. It was, however, an attempt, based on our experience of selfhood, to carry out the project of "faith seeking understanding" by proposing experiential analogies for illuminating the essential ideas of Christianity. I shall not, of course, attempt to recount what I wrote then, but a few examples will serve to indicate the line of thought I followed. In a chapter, "Man and the Circular Predicament," I sought to present the Christian diagnosis of the human situation and thus reinterpret the idea of sin. Understanding the person as unified by a purpose, what I called a "center of intention," I described God as the "transcending" center of intention, and Christ as the concrete manifestation of that intention in relation to the world—"God was in Christ reconciling the world unto Himself." Finally, I described the church as the Beloved Community which is the locus of transforming power in history, the power to resolve the circular human predicament. In short, I was showing in particular the religious meaning of theological concepts through analogies with episodes drawn from our own experience. Although he was far too negative in his insistence that metaphysics makes no contribution to religion, James was right in asking that theological doctrines—the omniscience of God, the atonement accomplished by Christ, the Incarnation, and others—be made relevant to experience.

Atonement, for example, seems very remote and inapplicable to human life when it is understood, not in terms of the power of sacrificial love, but as a legal transaction taking place in another realm in which a God of vengeance exacts a penalty from sinful creatures which is ultimately paid by an innocent person. In this reliance on experience I see no retreat from interpretation which is basically speculative in character nor any denigration of conceptual meaning such as we find in James at times and Bergson. Neville's final point about the importance of non-Western modes of experience is well taken, and I agree with him, especially about the need to pay more attention to Chinese thought. The latter is particularly relevant in view of the claim by such thinkers as Chung-ying Cheng that the Western pattern of abstract thought derivative from the Greek philosophers creates problems in the understanding of nature and human nature which are overcome in the concrete, experiential thinking of the Neo-Confucian tradition.

NOTES

1. One finds in the writings of theologians, philosophers, and historians numerous references to the "faith seeking understanding" approach as if its meaning were perfectly obvious. I do not believe that this is so; we need to be clear about what is meant by understanding, why it does not mean proof in the sense of the classical arguments for God's existence, and how faith with understanding differs from the faith with which we started out. In turn, it is essential to determine the meaning of the principle expressed in the phrase that always accompanies the *fides quaerens*—*credo ut intelligam* or "I believe in order that I may understand," sometimes expressed as "unless you believe you will not understand." In *The Analogy of Experience*, I devoted chapter 1, "The Classical Meaning of 'Faith Seeking Understanding'" (pp. 1–24) to a discussion of these and some related questions. That discussion is quite essential for a grasp of how experience figures in the process because I proposed that it be taken as a new approach to the understanding we are trying to achieve.

2. In the complete context of my statement, my aim was to show

that religion and philosophy are intertwined and that developments in each have repercussions for the other. In this case I was arguing that religion can serve as a goad to philosophy by keeping metaphysical issues in the foreground and thus forestalling the lapse of philosophy into purely technical questions of interest only to professional philosophers.

Publications of John E. Smith

BOOKS

Royce's Social Infinite. New York: Liberal Arts Press, 1950. Repr. Hamden, Conn.: Archon Books, 1969.

Value Convictions and Higher Education. New Haven, Conn.: The Hazen Foundation, 1958.

Jonathan Edwards: Treatise Concerning Religious Affections, edited with an Introduction, Works of Jonathan Edwards, Vol. II. New Haven, Conn.: Yale University Press, 1959. (General Editor, Vols. 3–9; General Editor Emeritus, Vols. 10–)

The Spirit of American Philosophy. New York: Oxford University Press, 1963; Paperback, Oxford: Galaxy Books, 1966; Rev. ed., Albany: State University of New York Press, 1983; Japanese trans., K. Matsunobu and O. Noda, Tamagawa University Press, 1980; Indonesian trans., Semangat Filsafat Amerika, Jakarta, Yayasan Sumber Agung, 1995.

(Editor) *The Philosophy of Religion*. New York: The Macmillan Co., 1965.

Religion and Empiricism. Aquinas Lecture. Milwaukee: Marquette University Press, 1967.

Experience and God. New York: Oxford University Press, 1968; Paperback, Galaxy Books, Oxford, 1973; reprinted with new Preface, New York: Fordham University Press, 1995; Polish trans., Doswiadczenie I Bog, Danuta Petsch, Instytut Wydawniczy, PAX, 1971.

(Editor) *Contemporary American Philosophy* (Second Series). London: George Allen & Unwin, 1970.

Themes in American Philosophy. New York: Harper & Row, 1970.

The Analogy of Experience: An Approach to Understanding Religious Truth. Warfield Lectures. New York: Harper & Row, 1973.

Purpose and Thought: The Meaning of Pragmatism. London: Hutchinson; New Haven, Conn.: Yale University Press, 1978; Rev. ed., Chicago: The University of Chicago Press, 1984; Chinese trans., *Mu ti yu ssu hsiang*, Taiwan, 1983.

(Editor, with F. Ferre and J. Kockelmans) *The Challenge of Religion:*

Contemporary Readings in the Philosophy of Religion. New York: The Seabury Press, 1983.

(Editor, with W. Kluback) *Josiah Royce: Selected Writings.* New York: Paulist Press, 1988.

America's Philosophical Vision. Chicago: The University of Chicago Press, 1992.

Jonathan Edwards: Puritan, Preacher, Philosopher. London: Geoffrey Chapman; Notre Dame, Ind.: University of Notre Dame Press, 1992.

Quasi-Religions: Humanism, Marxism, Nationalism. London: The Macmillan Press Ltd, 1994; New York, St. Martin's Press, 1995.

(Editor, with H. Stout and K. Minkema) *A Jonathan Edwards Reader.* New Haven and London: Yale University Press, 1995.

Translation

Kant's Weltanschauung, by Richard Kroner. Tübingen: J. C. B. Mohr, 1916 with revisions by author. Chicago: The University of Chicago Press, 1956.

ARTICLES IN BOOKS

"Religion and Theology in Peirce." In *Studies in the Philosophy of Charles Sanders Peirce.* Ed. Philip P. Weiner and Frederic H. Young. Cambridge, Mass.: Harvard University Press, 1952. Pp. 252–67.

"The Individual, the Religious Community, and the Symbol." In *Symbols and Values: An Initial Study.* Proceedings of the Thirteenth Symposium of the Conference on Science, Philosophy, and Religion. Ed. Lyman Bryson et al. New York: Harper & Bros., 1967. Pp. 155–72.

"When Should We Not Tell the Truth?" In *Great Moral Dilemmas in Literature, Past and Present.* Ed. Robert M. MacIver. New York: Harper & Bros., 1967. Pp. 47–60.

"Nietzsche: The Conquest of the Tragic Through Art." In *The Tragic Vision and the Christian Faith.* Ed. Nathan A. Scott. New York: Association Press, 1957. Pp. 211–37.

"The Question of Man." In *The Philosophy of Kant and Our Modern World.* Ed. Charles W. Hendel. New York: Liberal Arts Press, 1957. Pp. 3–24.

"History," "Existential Philosophy." In *A Handbook of Christian Theology.* Ed. Marvin Halverson. New York: Meridian, 1958.

Introduction. *Josiah Royce: The World and the Individual.* 2 vols. Repr. ed. New York: Dover, 1959. Pp. vii–xii.

"John Dewey: Philosopher of Experience." In *John Dewey and the Experi-*

mental Spirit in Philosophy: Four Lectures Delivered at Yale University Commemorating the Hundredth Anniversary of the Birth of John Dewey. Ed. Charles W. Hendel. New York: Liberal Arts Press, 1959. Pp. 93–119. (Also in *The Review of Metaphysics*, 13, No 1 [1959], 60–78.)

"Der philosophische Pragmatismus Amerikas." In *Amerikanische Gelehrtenwoche.* Munich: Ludwig Maximilians Universität, 1961. Pp. 69–75.

"Religion im heutigen Amerika." In *Amerikanische Gelehrtenwoche.* Munich: Ludwig Maximilians Universität, 1961. Pp. 61–67.

"Ultimate Concern and the Really Ultimate." In *Religious Experience and Truth.* Ed. Sidney Hook. New York: New York University Press, 1961. Pp. 65–69.

"Religionsphilosophie im 19. and 20. Jh." In *Die Religion in Geschichte und Gegenwart.* 7 vols. Tübingen: Mohr, 1965. Vol. VI, Sh–Z, columns 1299–1304 [Part III of the entry Vereinigte Staaten von Amerika].

"Paul Tillich." In *Thirteen for Christ.* Ed. Melville Harcourt. New York: Sheed & Ward, 1963. Pp. 65–82.

"Kant's Doctrine of Matter." In *The Concept of Matter.* Ed. Ernan McMullin. Notre Dame, Ind.: University of Notre Dame Press, 1963. Pp. 399–411.

"Philosophy of Physical Science in the Twentieth Century." With Henry Margenau. In *The Evolution of Science.* Ed. Guy S. Metraux and François Crouzet. New York: Mentor, 1963. Pp. 362–95. (Originally published in *The Journal of World History*, 4, No. 3 [1958], 639–67.)

"The Critique of Abstractions and the Scope of Reason." In *Process and Divinity: The Hartshorne Festschrift.* Ed. William Reese and Eugene Freeman. LaSalle, Ill.: Open Court, 1964. Pp. 19–45.

Foreword. *The Meaning of God in Human Experience* by William Ernest Hocking. Repr. ed. New Haven, Conn.: Yale University Press, 1963. Pp. vii–x.

"The Person: Solitude and Community." In *The Person in Contemporary Society: A Symposium on the Occasion of the Dedication of the Memorial Library, Notre Dame University, May 7, 1964.* Privately printed. Pp. 36–66.

"The Philosophy of Religion in America." In *Religion: Humanistic Scholarship in America.* The Princeton Series. Ed. Paul R. Ramsey. Englewood Cliffs, N.J.: Prentice Hall, 1965. Pp. 355–450.

Foreword. *Lectures on Modern Idealism* by Josiah Royce. Repr. ed. New Haven, Conn.: Yale University Press, 1964. Pp. vii–x.

"Die Amerikanische Philosophie seit Dewey." In *Amerika deutet sich selbst.* Ed. Peter Coulmas. Hamburg: Hoffman & Campse, 1965. Pp. 176–93.

"Community and Reality." In *Perspectives on Peirce*. Ed. R. J. Bernstein. New Haven, Conn.: Yale University Press, 1965. Pp. 92–119.

"The Philosophy of Religion." In *The Great Ideas Today*. Ed. Robert M. Hutchins and Mortimer J. Adler. Chicago: Encyclopedia Britannica, 1965. Pp. 212–53.

"Is the Self an Ultimate Category?" In *Philosophy, Religion, and the Coming World Civilization*. Ed. Leroy Rouner. The Hague: Martinus Nijhoff, 1966. Pp. 135–50.

"Josiah Royce." In *The Encyclopedia of Philosophy*. Vol. 7. Ed. Paul Edwards. New York: Macmillan, 1967. Pp. 225–29.

"The Experience of the Holy and the Idea of God." In *Phenomenology in America*. Ed. James Edie. Chicago: The University of Chicago Press, 1967. Pp. 295–306.

Foreword. *Charles S. Peirce on Norms and Ideals* by Vincent G. Potter, s.j. Amherst: University of Massachusetts Press, 1967. Pp. vii–viii. Repr. New York: Fordham University Press, 1997. Pp. xxv–xxvi.

"Absolutes, Ethical." "Rights." "Autonomy of Ethics." "Duty." In *A Dictionary of Christian Ethics*. Ed. John Macquarrie. Philadelphia: Westminster, 1967.

"Randall's Interpretation of the Role of Knowledge in Religion." In *Naturalism and Historical Understanding: Essays on the Philosophy of John Herman Randall, Jr.* Ed. John P. Anton. Albany: State University of New York Press, 1967. Pp. 250–63.

"Science and Religion: A Reappraisal." In *Science and Contemporary Society*. Ed. J. F. Crosson. Notre Dame, Ind.: University of Notre Dame Press, 1967. Pp. 155–74.

"The Individual and the Judeo-Christian Tradition." In *The Status of the Individual East and West*. Ed. C. A. Moore. Honolulu: University of Hawaii Press, 1968. Pp. 251–70.

"Radical Theology and the Theological Enterprise." In *New Themes in Christian Philosophy*. Ed. R. M. McInerny. Notre Dame, Ind.: Notre Dame University Press, 1968. Pp. 214–32.

"Hegel's Reinterpretation of the Doctrine of Spirit and the Religious Community." In *Hegel and the Philosophy of Religion*. Ed. Darrel E. Christensen. The Hague: Martinus Nijhoff, 1970. Pp. 157–77.

"Religion and Intelligence in Ministry." The Hoover Lectures. The University of Chicago, 1970. Privately printed.

"Religious Experience." In *Encyclopedia Britannica*. 15th ed. Chicago: Encyclopedia Britannica, 1974. Pp. 647–52.

"Creativity in Royce's Philosophical Idealism." In *Contemporary Studies in Philosophical Idealism*. Ed. J. Howie and T. O. Buford. West Dennis, Cape Cod, Mass.: Claude Stark & Co., 1975. Pp. 197–215.

Foreword. *The Culture of Experience* by John McDermott. New York: New York University Press, 1976. Pp. xvii–xx.

"Blanshard's Critique of Pragmatism." In *The Philosophy of Brand Blanshard.* Library of Living Philosophers 15. Ed. Paul A. Schilpp. LaSalle, Ill.: Open Court, 1977. Pp. 673–85.

"Nature as Object and as Environment." In *Nature and Man: Second Conference of the International Society for Metaphysics, Santiniketan, India.* Ed. George F. McLean. Calcutta: Oxford University Press, 1978. Pp. 50–57.

"Faith, Belief, and the Problem of Rationality in Religion." In *Rationality and Religious Belief: Proceedings of the Notre Dame Conference.* Ed. C. F. Delaney. Notre Dame, Ind.: University of Notre Dame Press, 1979. Pp. 42–64.

"Experience and the Boundary Between Philosophy and Religion." In *Philosophers on Their Own Work/(Philosophische Selbstbetrachtungen).* Fédération Internationale de Sociétés de Philosophie. Ed. André Mercier. Bern: Peter Lang, 1980. Pp. 191–237.

"Experience, Analogy, and Religious Insight." In *Experience, Reason, and God: Essays in the Philosophy of Religion.* Ed. Eugene Thomas Long. Studies in Philosophy and the History of Philosophy 8. Washington, D.C.: The Catholic University of America Press, 1980. Pp. 5–18.

"Receptivity, Change, and Relevance: Some Hallmarks of Philosophy in America." In *Two Centuries of Philosophy in America.* Ed. Peter Caws. APQ Library of Philosophy 7. Oxford: Basil Blackwell, 1980. Pp. 185–98.

"Hegel in St. Louis." In *Hegel's Social and Political Thought.* Ed. Donald Phillip Verene. Atlantic Highlands, N.J.: Humanities Press, 1980. Pp. 215–26.

"Religion Within the Scope of Philosophy." In *The History of Philosophy in the Making.* Ed. Linus J. Thro. Washington, D.C.: University Press of America, 1982. Pp. 247–54.

"Royce: The Absolute and the Beloved Community Revisited." In *Meaning, Truth, and God.* Ed. Leroy S. Rouner. Boston University Studies in Philosophy and Religion 3. Notre Dame, Ind., and London: Notre Dame University Press, 1982. Pp. 135–53.

"Community and Reality." In *The Relevance of Charles Peirce.* Ed. Eugene Freeman. LaSalle, Ill.: Open Court, 1983. Pp. 38–58.

"William James' Account of Mysticism: A Critical Appraisal." in *Mysticism and Religious Traditions.* Ed. Steven T. Katz. New York: Oxford Univeristy Press, 1983. Pp. 247–79.

"The New Need for a Recovery in Philosophy." In *The Spirit of American Philosophy.* Rev. ed. John E. Smith. Albany: State University of New

York Press, 1983. Pp. 223–42. Also Presidential Address, American Philosophical Association, Eastern Division, *Proceedings of the American Philosophical Association*, 56, No. 1 (1983), 5–18. Chinese translation: *Chinese Cultural Monthly*, 57 (1984), 15–32.

"Some Aspects of Hartshorne's Treatment of Anselm." In *Existence and Actuality: Conversations with Charles Hartshorne*. Ed. John B. Cobb. Chicago: The University of Chicago Press, 1984. Pp. 103–109.

"The Problem of Freedom in Contemporary Philosophy." In *Proceedings of the Fifth International Humanistic Symposium*. Athens: Hellenic Society for Humanistic Studies, 1984. Pp. 215–25.

"Some Continental and Marxist Approaches to Pragmatism." In *Contemporary Marxism*. Ed. James J. O'Rourke et al. The Hague: Reidel, 1984. Pp. 199–214.

"The Individual, the Collective, and the Community." In *The Philosophy of Gabriel Marcel*. Ed. Paul A. Schilpp and Lewis Hahn. The Library of Living Philosophers 17. LaSalle, Ill.: Open Court, 1984. Pp. 137–48.

Introduction. *The Varieties of Religious Experience* by William James. The Works of William James 15. Cambridge, Mass.: Harvard University Press. Pp. xi–li.

"William James and Josiah Royce." *Nineteenth-Century Religious Thought in the West* II. Ed. Ninian Smart et al. Cambridge: Cambridge University Press, 1985. Pp. 315–49.

"The Impact of Tillich's Interpretation of Religion." In *The Thought of Paul Tillich*. Ed. James Luther Adams, Wilhalm Pauck, and Roger Lincoln Shinn. San Francisco: Harper & Row, 1985. Pp. 240–59.

"The Meaning of Religious Experience in Hegel and Whitehead." In *Hegel and Whitehead*. Ed. George R. Lucas, Jr. Albany: State University of New York Press, 1986. Pp. 285–309.

"Jonathan Edwards and the Great Awakening." In *Doctrine and Experience*. Ed. Vincent G. Potter. New York: Fordham University Press, 1988. Pp. 7–21.

"Mediation, Conflict, and Creative Diversity." In *Harmony and Strife: Contemporary Perspectives East and West*. Ed. Shu-hsien Liu and Robert Allinson. Hong Kong: The Chinese University Press, 1988. Pp. 31–48.

"The Two Journeys to the Divine Presence." In *The Universe as Journey: Conversations with W. Norris Clarke, S.J.* Ed. Gerald A. McCool, s.j. New York: Fordham University Press, 1988. Pp. 131–50.

"Interpreting Across Boundaries." In *Understanding the Chinese Mind: The Philosophical Roots*. Ed. Robert E. Allinson. Hong Kong and New York: Oxford University Press, 1989. Pp. 26–47.

"Harris's Commentary on Hegel's *Logic.*" In *Dialectic and Contemporary Science*. Lanham, Md.: University Press of America, 1989. Pp. 55–64.
"Neoclassical Metaphysics and the History of Philosophy." In *The Philosophy of Charles Hartshorne*. Ed. Lewis Edwin Hahn. The Library of Living Philosophers 20. Chicago and LaSalle, Ill.: Open Court, 1991. Pp. 498–507.
"Two Perspectives on Friendship: Aristotle and Nietzsche." In *The Changing Face of Friendship*. Ed. Leroy S. Rouner. Boston University Studies in Philosophy and Religion 15. Notre Dame, Ind.: Notre Dame University Press, 1994. Pp. 57–73.
"Puritanism and Enlightenment." In *Knowledge and Belief in America*. Ed. William M. Shea and Peter A. Huff. Washington, D.C.: Woodrow Wilson Center Press; Cambridge: Cambridge University Press, 1995. Pp. 195–226.
"Freud, Philosophy, and Interpretation." In *The Philosophy of Paul Ricoeur*. Ed. Lewis Edwin Hahn. The Library of Living Philosophers 22. Chicago and LaSalle, Ill.: Open Court, 1995. Pp. 147–64.

ARTICLES IN JOURNALS

"Professor Weiss, 'Existenz' and Hegel." *Philosophy and Phenomenological Research*, 9, No. 2 (1948), 322–25.
"The Christian Answer: A Review Article." *The Review of Religion*, 12, No. 2 (1948), 150–57.
"Religion and Morality." *The Journal of Religion*, 29, No. 2 (1949), 85–94.
"Kant, Paton, and Beck." *The Review of Metaphysics*, 3, No. 2 (1949), 229–48.
"Is Existence a Valid Philosophical Concept?" *The Journal of Philosophy*, 47 (1950), 238–49.
"Royce on Religion." *The Journal of Religion*, 30, No. 3 (1950), 261–65.
"Existence, the Past, and God." *The Review of Metaphysics*, 6, No. 2 (1952), 287–95.
"Beyond Realism and Idealism: An Appreciation of W. M. Urban." *The Review of Metaphysics*, 6, No. 3 (1953), 337–50.
"The Revolt of Existence." *Yale Review*, 63, No. 3 (1954), 364–71.
"Rousseau, Romanticism, and the Philosophy of Existence." *Yale French Studies*, 13, No. 1 (1954), 52–61.
"Hartmann's New Ontology." *The Review of Metaphysics*, 7, No. 4 (1954), 583–601.
"Poetry, Religion, and Theology." *The Review of Metaphysics*, 9, No. 2 (1955), 252–73.

"The Task of the Christian in Philosophy." *The Christian Scholar*, 39, No. 2 (1956), 88–101.

"Tre tipi e due dogmi dell'empirismo." *Revista di Filosofia*, 68, No. 3 (1957), 257–73.

"The Course of American Philosophy." *The Review of Metaphysics*, 9, No. 2 (1957), 279–303. Reprinted in *Japanese Americana*, 4, No. 6 (1958), 71–92.

"The University: 'An Association of Masters and Scholars'" (The Ralph Hill Thomas Lecture). *Yale Alumni Magazine*, 22, No. 2 (1958), 8–11.

"The Present Status of Natural Theology." *The Journal of Philosophy*, 55, No. 22 (1958), 925–36.

"The Experiential Foundations of Religion." *The Journal of Philosophy*, 55, No. 13 (1958), 538–46.

"Philosopher on Tillich." *The Christian Century*, 75, No. 49 (1958), 1399–1401.

"Knowledge of Selves and the Theory of Interpretation." *Kantstudien*, 5, No. 3 (1959), 315–21.

"John Dewey: Philosopher of Experience." *The Review of Metaphysics*, 13, No. 1 (1959), 60–78.

"The Impact of Wittgenstein." *The Christian Scholar*, 43, No. 3 (1960), 239–44.

"Three Types and Two Dogmas of Empiricism." *The Christian Scholar*, 63, No. 3 (1960), 199–212.

"Christianity and Philosophy: The Problem of a Christian Philosophy." *The Journal of Religious Thought*, 17, No. 2 (1960), 67–85.

"Science and Religion: Must They Exclude Each Other?" *Yale Scientific Magazine*, 35, No. 3 (1960), 20–26.

"La libertà umana e alcune concezioni scientifiche." *Revista di Filosofia*, 52, No. 2 (1961), 139–55.

"The Permanent Truth in the Idea of Natural Religion" (The Dudleian Lecture for 1960). *Harvard Theological Review*, 54, No. 1 (1961), 1–19.

"The Gap Between Science and Ethics." *Yale Alumni Magazine*, 24, No. 8 (1961), 15–19.

"Philosophy in America Today." *Occasional Papers of the Rockefeller Institute* (1961) (13 pp).

"Purpose in American Philosophy." *International Philosophical Quarterly*, 1, No. 3 (1961), 390–406.

"The Concept of the Moral, Moral Relativism, the Nature of Moral Norms and the Sources of Moral Authority." *Religious Education*, 57, No. 6 (1962), 445–48.

"The Moral Situation." *Religious Education*, 58, No. 2 (1963), 106–14.

"The Relation of Thought and Being: Some Lessons From Hegel's *Encyclopedia.*" *The New Scholasticism,* 38 (1964), 22–43.

"The Encounter Between Philosophy and Religion" (The Suarez Lecture, Fordham University). *Thought,* 39, No. 152 (1964), 20–36.

"The Concept of Logos and the Theological Enterprise." *Union Seminary Quarterly Review,* 20, No. 2 (1965), 149–64.

"Radical Empiricism." *Proceedings of the Aristotelian Society,* 65 (1965) 205–18.

"The Structure of Religion." *Religious Studies,* 1, No. 1 (1965), 63–73.

"Representative Thinkers in the Development of American Philosophy." *The Barat Review,* 2, No. 1 (1967), 3–12.

"Anselm's Discovery: A Re-Examination of the Ontological Proof for God's Existence." *The Journal of Religion,* 47, No. 4 (1967), 363–65.

"Religion and Morality." *Ararat* (Spring 1967), 42–51.

"The Contemporary Significance of Royce's Theory of the Self." *Revue Internationale de Philosophie,* 79–80 (1967), 77–89.

"Recent Work of J. N. Findlay." *Religious Studies,* 4 (1968), 275–82.

"William James as Philosophical Psychologist." *Midway,* 8, No. 3 (1968) 3–20.

"The Reflexive Turn, the Linguistic Turn, and the Pragmatic Outcome." *The Monist,* 53, No. 4 (1969), 588–605.

"The Inescapable Ambiguity of Nonviolence." *Philosophy East and West,* 19, No. 2 (1969), 155–58.

"Time, Times, and the 'Right Time.'" *The Monist,* 53, No. 1 (1969), 1–13.

"Self and World as Starting Points in Theology." *International Journal for Philosophy of Religion,* 1, No. 2 (1970), 97–111.

"In What Sense Can We Speak of Experiencing God?" *The Journal of Religion,* 50, No. 3 (1970), 229–44.

"Being, Immediacy, and Articulation." *The Review of Metaphysics,* 24, No. 4 (1971), 593–613. Presidential Address, Metaphysical Society of America, 1971.

"Religious Insight and the Cognitive Problem." *Religious Studies,* 7 (1971), 97–112.

"The Reality of God and the Denial of God." *The Journal of Religion,* 51, No. 2 (1971), 83–102. Presidential Address, American Theological Society, 1968.

"From Tension to Community—A Fresh Approach to the Teaching–Learning Situation." *Faculty Forum,* 58, Nos. 3–4; 59, Nos. 1–2, 5 (1972).

"History of Science and the Ideal of Scientific Objectivity." *Revue Internationale de Philosophie,* 99–100 (1972), 172–86.

"The Significance of Karl Barth's Thought for the Relation Between Philosophy and Theology." *Union Seminary Quarterly Review*, 28, No. 1 (1972), 15–30.

"Hegel's Critique of Kant." *The Review of Metaphysics*, 26, No. 3 (1973), 438–60. Reprinted in *Hegel and the History of Philosophy*. Ed. Joseph J. O'Malley et al. The Hague: Martinus Nijhoff, 1974. Pp. 108–28.

"The Scientific Enterprise and the Scientific Outlook." *Yale Scientific*, 48, No. 5 (1973), 14–20.

"Commentary on Henry Rosemont, Jr.'s Article, 'On Representing Abstractions in Archaic Chinese.'" *Philosophy East and West*, 24, No. 1 (1974), 95–97.

"Jonathan Edwards: Piety and Practice in the American Character." *The Journal of Religion*, 54, No. 2 (1974), 166–80.

"Commentary on J. L. Mehta's 'The Problem of Philosophical Reconception in the Thought of K. C. Bhattacharyya.'" *Philosophy East and West*, 24, No. 1 (1974), 89–93.

"Royce and Dewey on Community." *Southern Journal of Philosophy*, 12, No. 4 (1974), 469–79. Reprinted in *Civil Religion in America*, Dickinson College 200th Anniversary Symposium, Carlisle, Penn.: Dickinson College, 1975. Pp. 49–64.

"Some Comments on Cassirer's Interpretation of Religion." *Revue Internationale de Philosophie*, 110, No. 4 (1974) 475–91.

"Jonathan Edwards as Philosophical Theologian." *The Review of Metaphysics*, 30, No. 2 (1976), 306–24.

"Philosophical Ideas Behind the 'Declaration of Independence.'" *Revue Internationale de Philosophie*, 121–122 (1977), 360–76.

"Three-Dimensional Education." *Teacher's College Record*, 80, No. 3 (1979), 556–63. Reprinted in *Education and Values*. Ed. Douglas Sloan. New York: Teachers College Press, 1980. Pp. 160–67.

"Into the Secular Void: Cults and Charismatic Figures." *Commonweal*, March 16, 1979, pp. 139–40.

"Comments on Beth J. Singer's 'John E. Smith on Pragmatism,'" *Transactions of the Charles S. Peirce Society*, 16, No. 10 (1980), 14–33.

"The Religious Dimension of Human Life." *The Scottish Journal of Religious Studies*, 1, No. 1 (1980), 16–25.

"Science and Conscience." *American Scientist*, 68, No. 5 (1980), 554–58.

"The Tension Between Direct Experience and Argument in Religion." *Religious Studies*, 17 (1981), 487–98.

"A Fifty-Year Retrospective in Philosophy." *International Philosophical Quarterly*, 21 (1981), 123–32. Reprinted in 1985 by the Department of Philosophy, Jianxi University, Nanchang, China.

"Comments on Charles Courtney's 'Restructuring the Structure of Religion.'" *Logos*, 2 (1981), 83–84.

"Philosophical Interpretation and the Religious Dimension of Experience." *Logos*, 2 (1981), 5–20.

"Testing the Spirits: Jonathan Edwards and the Religious Affections." Essays in Honor of James A. Martin, Jr., 1982. *Union Seminary Quarterly Review*, 37, Nos. 1–2 (1982) 27–37.

"Community, Cooperation and the Adventure of Learning." *Soundings*, 65, No. 4 (1982), 447–55.

"Chung-ying Cheng on the Challenge of Chinese Philosophy." *Journal of Chinese Philosophy*, 11, No. 1 (1984), 13–19.

"The External and the Internal Odyssey of God in the Twentieth Century." *Religious Studies*, 20, No. 1 (1984), 43–54.

"Comments on A. S. Cua's 'Confucian Vision and Human Community.'" *Journal of Chinese Philosophy*, 11 (1984), 239–42.

"Tolerance as Principle and as Necessity." *Union Seminary Quarterly Review*, 38, Nos. 3–4 (1984), 289–300.

"The Reconception of Experience in Peirce, James, and Dewey." *The Monist*, 68, No. 4 (1985), 538–54.

"Pragmatism at Work: Dewey's Lectures in China." *The Journal of Chinese Philosophy*, 12, No. 3 (1985), 231–59.

"Time and Qualitative Time." *The Review of Metaphysics*, 60, No. 1 (1986), 3–16.

"Response" to "John E. Smith as an Interpreter of American Philosophy: A Symposium." *Transactions of the Charles S. Peirce Society*, 22, No. 3 (1986), 239–88.

"Some Pragmatic Tendencies in the Thought of Wang-yang Ming." *Journal of Chinese Philosophy*, 13 (1986), 167–83.

"The Fact of Religion: Diagnosis and Deliverance." *Scottish Journal of Religious Studies*, 6, No. 4 (1986), 61–77.

"Tillich, Being, and Biblical Religion." *Soundings*, 69, No. 4 (1986), 401–22.

"Herbert Schneider on the History of American Philosophy." *Journal of the History of Philosophy*, 25, No. 1 (1987), 169–77.

"Two Defenses of Freedom: Peirce and James." *Tulane Studies in Philosophy*, 35 (1987), 51–64.

"Pragmatism's Shared Metaphysical Vision: A Symposium on Sandra Rosenthal's *Speculative Pragmatism*." *Transactions of the Charles S. Peirce Society*, 23, No. 2 (1987), 351–60.

"Being and Willing: The Foundation of Ethics." *Journal of Speculative Philosophy*, N.S. 1, No. 1 (1987), 24–37.

"Conscience: The Lost Dimension in Education." CRIS [The Council for Religion in Independent Schools], *Occasional Papers in Religion and Ethics*, No. 2 (1990), 1–13.

"Blanshard on Philosophical Style." *Idealist Studies*, 20, No. 2 (1990), 100–11.

"An Open Letter to Charles Hartshorne." *The Journal of Speculative Philosophy*, 6, No. 4 (1992), 257–58.

"Prospects for Natural Theology." *The Monist*, 75, No. 3 (1992), 406–20.

"Person to Person—The Community and the Person." *Personalist Forum*, 8, No. 1 (1992), 41–54.

"Hegel and the Hegel Society of America." *The Owl of Minerva* (Twenty-Fifth Anniversary Edition), 25, No. 2 (1994), 135–40.

"Philosophy and Religion: One Central Reflection." *The International Journal for Philosophy of Religion* (Twenty-Fifth Anniversary Edition), 38 (1995), 103–108.

BOOK REVIEWS

Review of *Alfred Loisy: His Religious Significance*, by M. D. Petre (Cambridge and New York, 1944), in *Review of Religion*, 9, No. 4 (1945), 391–96.

Review of *Under Orders* by William L. Sullivan (New York, 1944), in *The Review of Religion*, 9, No. 4 (1945), 391–96.

Review of *A Kierkegaard Anthology*, ed. by R. Bretall (Princeton, 1946); *The Concept of Dread*, by Søren Kierkegaard, trans. W. Lowrie (Princeton, 1944), *Works of Love*, trans. David F. Swenson and Lillian M. Swenson (Princeton, 1946), *Attack Upon Christendom*, trans. W. Lowrie (Princeton, 1944), in *The Germanic Review*, 22, No. 3 (1947), 233–38.

Review of *Language and Myth*, by Ernst Cassirer, trans. Susanne Langer (New York, 1946), in *The Review of Religion*, 12 (November 1947), 82–87.

Review of *Early Theological Writings*, by Georg W. F. Hegel, trans. R. M. Knox, trans. Richard Kroner (Chicago, 1948), in *The Review of Religion*, 14, No. 2 (1950), 183–89.

Review of *The Good Life*, by E. Jordan (Chicago, 1949), in *The Review of Metaphysics*, 4, No. 4 (1951), 575–94.

Review of *A Short History of Existentialism*, by Jean Wahl, trans. F. Williams and S. Maron (New York, 1949), *The Philosophy of Existence*, by Gabriel Marcel, trans. M. Harari (New York, 1949), *The Perennial Scope of Philosophy*, by Karl Jaspers, trans. R. Manheim (New York, 1949), in *The Review of Religion*, 15, No. 3 (1951), 187–93.

PUBLICATIONS OF JOHN E. SMITH

Review of *The Theology of Paul Tillich*, ed. Charles Kegley and Robert Bretall (New York, 1952), in *The Journal of Philosophy*, 50, No. 21 (1952), 638–46.

Review of *Dialectic*, by Gustav Mueller (New York, 1953), in *The Review of Religion*, 19, Nos. 1–2 (1954), 80–85.

Review of *Against the Stream: Shorter Post-War Writings, 1946–1952*, by Karl Barth (New York, 1954), in *The Journal of Philosophy*, 51, No. 5 (1955), 131–34.

Review of *Royce on the Human Self*, by J. Harry Cotton (Cambridge, 1954), in *The Philosophical Review*, 65, No. 3 (1956), 420–24.

Review of *Approaches to God*, by Jacques Maritain, trans. Peter O'Reilly, ed. Ruth Nanda Anshen (New York, 1954), in *The Review of Religion*, 20, Nos. 3–4 (1956), 207–11.

Review of *The Energies of Art: Studies of Authors, Classic and Modern*, by Jacques Barzun (New York, 1957), in "The Critic as Thinker," *Yale Review*, 66, No. 2 (1957), 267–70.

Review of *Ludwig Wittgenstein*, by Norman Malcolm (London, 1958), in "The Impact of Wittgenstein," *The Christian Scholar*, 63 (Fall 1960), 3–7.

Review of *Herman Schell als existentieller Denker und Theologe*, by Joseph Hasenfuss (Wurzburg, 1956), *Erasmus: Speculum Scientiarum*, 14, No. 13–14 (1961), 394–98.

Review of *Dynamics of Faith*, by Paul Tillich (New York, 1967), *Theology of Culture*, ed. R. C. Kimball (New York, 1959), in *The Journal of Philosophy*, 58, No. 15 (1961), 412–15.

Review of *Reason and Life: The Introduction to Philosophy*, by Julian Marias, trans. Kenneth Reid and Edward Sarmiento (New Haven, 1956), in *The Journal of Philosophy*, 58, No. 20 (1961), 600–602.

Review of *Hegel: A Re-examination*, by J. N. Findlay (London and New York, 1958), in *Hegel-Studien*, 1 (1961), 326–34.

Review of *The Logic of Perfection*, by Charles Hartshorne (LaSalle, Ill., 1962), in *The Chicago Theological Seminary Register*, 53, No. 5 (1962), 41–43.

Review of *Moral and Beyond*, by Paul Tillich (New York 1963), in "Ethics, Love and Wisdom," *Saturday Review*, 67 (1964), 80.

Review of *The Moral Philosophy of Josiah Royce*, by Peter Fuss (Cambridge, Mass., 1965), in *The Philosophical Review*, 76, No. 4 (1967), 515–19.

Review of *The Letters of William James and Theodore Flournoy*, ed. R. C. LeClair (Madison, Milwaukee, and London), in *The New England Quarterly*, 40, No. 3 (1967), 476–79.

Review of *In Search of Philosophic Understanding*, by E. A. Burtt (New

York and Toronto, 1965), in *The Philosophical Review*, 78, No. 1 (1969), 99–102.

Review of *The Perfectibility of Man*, by John Passmore (New York, 1971), in *The Philosophical Review*, 80, No. 3 (1972), 394–401.

Review of *Theopoetic Theology and the Religious Imagination*, by Amos Wilder (Philadelphia, 1976), in *Religious Studies*, 17 (1979), 106–109.

Review of *Omnipotence and Other Theological Mistakes*, by Charles Hartshorne (Albany, 1983), in *Faith and Philosophy*, 1, No. 4 (1984), 437–39.

Review of *An Interpretation of Hegel's Logic*, by Errol E. Harris (Lanham, Md., 1983), in *British Journal for the Philosophy of Science*, 36 (1985), 461–65.

Review of *Charles S. Peirce's Evolutionary Philosophy*, by Carl R. Hausman (Cambridge, 1993), *International Philosophical Quarterly*, 35, No. 3 (1995), 347–49.

Review of *Peirce's Philosophical Perspectives*, by Vincent G. Potter, ed. Vincent M. Colapietro (New York, 1996), in *International Philosophical Quarterly*, 37, No. 2 (June 1997), 225–30.